SECOND EDITION

TOP NOTCH

English for Today's World

3A

WITH WORKBOOK

Joan Saslow • Allen Ascher

With *Top Notch Pop Songs and Karaoke*
by Rob Morsberger

Top Notch: English for Today's World 3, Second Edition

Copyright © 2011 by Pearson Education, Inc.
All rights reserved. No part of this publication may be reproduced, stored in a retrieval system, or transmitted in any form or by any means, electronic, mechanical, photocopying, recording, or otherwise, without the prior permission of the publisher.

Pearson Education, 10 Bank Street, White Plains, NY 10606

Staff credits: The people who made up the Top Notch 3 team—representing editorial, design, production, and manufacturing—are Rhea Banker, Peter Benson, Elizabeth Carlson, Aerin Csigay, Dave Dickey, Warren Fischbach, Shelley Gazes, Aliza Greenblatt, Ray Keating, and Mike Kemper.

Photo credits: All original photography by Sharon Hoogstraten and David Mager. Page 2 (background) Shutterstock.com, (top left) Will & Deni McIntyre/Getty Images, (top middle left) Robert Frerck/Odyssey Productions, Inc., (top middle right) Michael Goldman/Masterfile, (top right) Jeff Greenberg/PhotoEdit Inc., (bottom left) Michael Newman/PhotoEdit Inc., (bottom middle left) Dorling Kindersley; p. 5 Shutterstock.com; p. 7 (Egypt) Dallas & John Heaton/Corbis, (Mexico) John Neubauer/PhotoEdit Inc., (China) Picture Finders Ltd./eStock Photo, (Peru) Renee Comet Photography/Stockfood America, (Japan) Dallas & John Heaton/Corbis, (Rio) Mathias Oppersdorff/Photo Researchers, Inc., (Feijoada) Mourad Tarek/Stockfood America; p. 8 (middle) Shutterstock.com, (bottom) Shutterstock.com; p. 10 (middle) Shutterstock.com, (1) Shutterstock.com, (2) Shutterstock.com, (3) Shutterstock.com; p. 11 Sunstar/Photo Researchers, Inc.; p. 12 (1) Renee Comet Photography/Stockfood America, (2) Steve Vidler/eStock Photo, (3) Superstock, (4) Rafael Macia/Photo Researchers, Inc.; p. 14 (left) Warner Bros/Photofest, (middle left) Photofest, (middle right) DreamWorks/Photofest, (right) Paramount Pictures/Photofest; p. 16 Stephane Cardinale/People Avenue/Corbis; p. 18 (action) Original Films/Bob Marshak/The Kobal Collection, (horror) Warner Bros/The Kobal Collection, (sci-fi) MGM/The Kobal Collection, (animated) Globe Photos, (comedy) Morgan Creek/The Kobal Collection, (drama) Paramount/The Kobal Collection, (documentary) Les Gibbon/Alamy, (musical) Simon Fergusson/Getty Images; p. 20 Shutterstock.com, (top right) Shutterstock.com, (bottom left) Shutterstock.com, (bottom middle) Shutterstock.com; p. 22 Shutterstock.com; p. 23 Miramax Films/Photofest; p. 26 (top right logos) Shutterstock.com, (single) Jeff Greenberg/PhotoEdit Inc., (double) Jeff Greenberg/PhotoEdit Inc.; p. 28 Shutterstock.com; p. 30 Shutterstock.com, (top right) Inspirestock RF/Getty Images; p. 32 (towels) Comstock.com, (hangers) Jose Luis Pelaez, Inc./Corbis, (iron) Michael Matisse/Getty Images, (dryer) Getty Images, (make up) Jeff Greenberg/Index Stock Imagery, (turn down) Comstock.com, (bring up) David Bartruff Inc.; p. 33 Shutterstock.com; p. 34 (left) Dorling Kindersley, (middle) Rudy Van Briel/PhotoEdit Inc., (right) Bernard Boutrit/Woodfin Camp Associates; p. 37 (left) Shutterstock.com, (right) Shutterstock.com; p. 38 (left) Shutterstock.com, (sedan) Courtesy DaimlerChrysler Corporation, (compact) Shutterstock.com, (wagon) Dorling Kindersley, (van) David Young-Wolff/PhotoEdit Inc., (convertible) David Young-Wolff/PhotoEdit Inc., (SUV) Kurt Wittman/Corbis, (sports) Adam Woolfitt/Corbis, (luxury) Ron Kimball Photography; p. 44 (bottom right) Shutterstock.com; p. 45 (Lexor) Photolibrary.com, (Sea) Ron Kimball Photography; (Outing) Izmostock/Alamy, (Invocation) Photolibrary.com, (Turbo) Photolibrary.com, (Micro) Dreamstime.com, (Amigo) Shutterstock.com, (Overland) Izmostock/Alamy; p. 46 iStockphoto.com; p. 47 Shutterstock.com; p. 50 (top left) Shutterstock.com, (top middle) Shutterstock.com, (top right) Shutterstock.com, (bottom left) Shutterstock.com, (bottom middle) Photolibrary.com, (bottom right) Shutterstock.com; p. 52 (2) Shutterstock.com, (4) Helene Rogers/Alamy, (6) Shutterstock.com, (7) Shutterstock.com, (8) Shutterstock.com, (10) Shutterstock.com, (12) Shutterstock.com, (13) Shutterstock.com, (14) Shutterstock.com, (15) Shutterstock.com, (16) Shutterstock.com; p. 56 (left) Shutterstock.com, (right) Michael Bermant, MD, Board Certified, American Board of Plastic Surgery, www.plasticsurgery4u.com; p. 57 Bill Losh/Getty Images; p. 58 (left) Shutterstock.com, (right) Shutterstock.com; p. 59 (1) Shutterstock.com, (2) Shutterstock.com, (3) Shutterstock.com; p. 62 (fats) Shutterstock.com, (meat) Shutterstock.com, (dairy) Shutterstock.com, (fruit) Shutterstock.com, (vegetables) Shutterstock.com, (breads) Shutterstock.com; p. 64 (sushi) Vito Arcomano/eStock Photo, (mangoes) Dorey Cardinale Photography/Stockfood America, (pasta) Thom DeSanto Photography, Inc./Stockfood America, (ice cream) Judd Pilossof/FoodPix, (asparagus) Andy Ryan Photography/Stockfood America; p. 67 (shellfish) Geoffrey Clifford/Woodfin Camp Associates, (chocolates) Renee Comet Photography/Stockfood America, (tofu) Gary Conner/PhotoEdit Inc., (steak) Renee Comet Photography/Stockfood America, (fries) Maximilian Stock/Stockfood America, (noodles) Alan Campbell Productions/Stockfood America, (sardines) Maximilian Stock/Stockfood America; p. 68 (left) Photolibrary.com, (right) Photolibrary.com; p. 69 Shutterstock.com; p. 70 (a left) Jimmy Dorantes/LatinFocus.com, (a right) George D. Lepp/Corbis, (b) Michael Newman/PhotoEdit Inc., (c) Steve Cohen/FoodPix, (d) Foodcollection/Stockfood America, (e) David Young-Wolff/PhotoEdit Inc., (f left) Cathy Melloan/PhotoEdit Inc., (f right) Gary White Photography/Stockfood America; p. 71 (top) Dorling Kindersley, (right) Michael Newman/PhotoEdit, Inc.; p. 73 (background) Tyson Foods, Inc., (Thailand) Stephen Mark Needham/Foodpix, (Korea) James Baigrie/Foodpix, (Mexico) Jimmy Dorantes/LatinFocus.com, (Colombia) Henry Rodríguez Bohórquez, (Lebanon) James Baigrie/Getty Images, (China) Shutterstock.com, (Peru) Veronica Vallarino; p. 74 Shutterstock.com; p. 76 Photolibrary.com; p. 80 Shutterstock.com; p. 81 (top) David Muir/Masterfile, (bottom right) Shutterstock.com; p. 82 Ken Weingart/ImageState; p. 83 (top) Tony Freeman/PhotoEdit Inc., (bottom) Anthony Redpath/Corbis; p. 85 (background) Dimitri Vervitsiotis/Getty Images, (middle) Photos.com, (bottom) David Butlow/Corbis; p. 86 (drawing) A. Ascher "Talavera", (jewelry) Wendy Wolf "tagua nut, Bayong wood, and lava rock necklace", (fashion) Shutterstock.com, (sculpture) Vivian Nash "La Rueda", (pottery) Matthew J. Sovjani "Wave Vase", (painting) Jessica Miller-Smith "Rockefeller Preserve", (photography) Peter C. Benson "Sagamore"; p. 87 (top) Mrs. Simon Guggenheim Fund. (163.1945). ®2004 Successió Miro/Artist Rights Society ARS, NY. The Museum of Modern Art/Licensed by Scala-Art Resource, NY, (bottom) Historical Picture Archive/Corbis; p. 89 (top) Francis G. Mayer/Corbis, (David) Copyright ©2001 by Martin Yu, (K'uan) Collection of the National Palace Museum, Taiwan, Republic of China, (Rivera) Reproduction authorized by the Instituto Nacional de Bellas Artes y Literatura. Courtesy of Art Resource, NY; p. 90 (wood) Paul A. Souders/Corbis, (glass) Susan Van Etten/PhotoEdit Inc., (silver) Charles Edenshaw. Photograph by Paul Macapia. Seattle Art Museum, (gold) Art Resource, NY, (cloth) Iconotec/Alamy, (clay) Stockbyte, (stone) Banco Mexicano de Imagenes/The Bridgeman Art Library International Ltd., p. 91 (top) Lizz Carlson, (pot) Shutterstock.com, (vase) Picture Desk, Inc./Kobal Collection (dolls) Dave G. Houser/Corbis, (figure) Cluadia Obrocki/Art Resource, NY, (cups) Shutterstock.com; p. 92 Audrey Benson; p. 94 (top left) The Newark Museum/Art Resource, NY, (top right) Art Resource, NY, (middle) Reuters NewMedia Inc./Corbis, (bottom left) Bettmann/Corbis, (bottom middle) Reuters/Corbis, (bottom right) Stephane Cardinale/People Avenue/Corbis; p. 95 (right) Shutterstock.com; p. 96 (a) Collier Campbell Lifeworks/Corbis, (b) Heini Schneebeli/The Bridgeman Art Library International Ltd., (c) Erich Lessing/Art Resource, NY, (d) Archivo Iconografico, S.A./Corbis, (e) Picture Desk, Inc./Kobal Collection; p. 97 (background) Shutterstock.com, (Louvre) Richard List/Corbis, (Mona) Gianni Dagli Orti/Corbis, (Tate) Shutterstock.com, (Mustard) Tate Gallery, London/Art Resource, NY, (Japan) Sakamoto Photo Research Laboratory/Corbis, (Peru) Mireille Vautier/Woodfin Camp & Associates, (France) Picture Desk, Inc./Kobal Collection, (Mexico) Corbis; p. 98 (top) Shutterstock.com, (monitor) Burke/Triolo/Jupiterimages, (keyboard) Shutterstock.com, (mouse) Shutterstock.com, (touchpad) Shutterstock.com, (bottom) Shutterstock.com; p. 100 (background) Shutterstock.com, (hand) Shutterstock.com; p. 101 Fotolia.com; p. 102 Logitech, Inc.; p. 104 (4) Shutterstock.com; p. 106 Burke/Triolo/Jupiterimages, p. 109 (background) Shutterstock.com, (family photo) Shutterstock.com; p. 115 (wallet) Dorling Kindersley, (books) Myrleen Ferguson Cate/PhotoEdit Inc., (phone) Shutterstock.com, (jacket) Dorling Kindersley, (glove) Dorling Kindersley, (umbrella) Shutterstock.com, (suitcase) Dorling Kindersley; p. 116 (left) Robert Rathe/Mira.com, (middle) Shutterstock.com, (right) Shutterstock.com; p. 117 Library of Congress; p. 118 Shutterstock.com.

Illustration credits: Steve Attoe, pp. 6, 64; Sue Carlson, p. 35; John Ceballos, pp. 25, 37, 49, 121; Mark Collins, pp. 27, 42 (left); John Hovell, p. 9; Brian Hughes, pp. 24 (bottom), 41, 71; Adam Larkum, p. 61; Pat Lewis, p. 10; Andy Myer, pp. 16 (left, center), 66, 106; Dusan Petricic, pp. 8, 33, 41, 70, 78, 79, 113; Jake Rickwood, p. 24 (top); Neil Stewart, p. 119 (center, bottom); Anne Veltfort, pp. 16 (right), 29, 42 (right), 66 (top-right), 119 (top); Jean Wisenbaugh, p. 13.

Text credits: Page 46 (article) Teens Health.org, (c) 2007–2009, Adapted with permission; p.74 Information Please® 2009 Pearson, Inc. All rights reserved.

Printed in the United States of America

ISBN 10 : 0-13-246987-1
ISBN 13 : 978-0-13-246987-6
6 7 8 9 10 - V042 - 17 16 15 14 13 12

ISBN 10 : 0-13-247027-6 (with MyEnglishLab)
ISBN 13 : 978-0-13-247027-8 (with MyEnglishLab)
1 2 3 4 5 6 7 8 9 10 - V042 - 17 16 15 14 13 12

About the Authors

Joan Saslow

Joan Saslow has taught in a variety of programs in South America and the United States. She is author of a number of multi-level integrated-skills courses for adults and young adults: *Ready to Go: Language, Lifeskills, and Civics; Workplace Plus: Living and Working in English;* and of *Literacy Plus*. She is also author of *English in Context: Reading Comprehension for Science and Technology*. Ms. Saslow was the series director of *True Colors* and *True Voices*. She participates in the English Language Specialist Program in the U.S. Department of State's Bureau of Educational and Cultural Affairs.

Allen Ascher

Allen Ascher has been a teacher and a teacher trainer in China and the United States and taught in the TESOL Certificate Program at the New School in New York. He was also academic director of the International English Language Institute at Hunter College. Mr. Ascher is author of the "Teaching Speaking" module of *Teacher Development Interactive*, an online multimedia teacher-training program, and of *Think about Editing: A Grammar Editing Guide for ESL*.

Both Ms. Saslow and Mr. Ascher are frequent and popular speakers at professional conferences and international gatherings of EFL and ESL teachers.

Authors' Acknowledgments

The authors are indebted to these reviewers who provided extensive and detailed feedback and suggestions for the second edition of *Top Notch* as well as the hundreds of teachers who participated in surveys and focus groups.

Manuel Aguilar Díaz, El Cultural Trujillo, Peru • **Manal Al Jordi,** Expression Training Company, Kuwait • **José Luis Ames Portocarrero,** El Cultural Arequipa, Peru • **Vanessa de Andrade,** CCBEU Inter Americano, Curitiba, Brazil • **Rossana Aragón Castro,** ICPNA Cusco, Peru • **Jennifer Ballesteros,** Universidad del Valle de México, Campus Tlalpan, Mexico City, Mexico • **Brad Bawtinheimer,** PROULEX, Guadalajara, Mexico • **Carolina Bermeo,** Universidad Central, Bogotá, Colombia • **Zulma Buitrago,** Universidad Pedagógica Nacional, Bogotá, Colombia • **Fabiola R. Cabello,** Idiomas Católica, Lima, Peru • **Emma Campo Collante,** Universidad Central Bogotá, Colombia • **Viviane de Cássia Santos Carlini,** Spectrum Line, Pouso Alegre, Brazil • **Fanny Castelo,** ICPNA Cusco, Peru • **José Luis Castro Moreno,** Universidad de León, Mexico • **Mei Chia-Hong,** Southern Taiwan University (STUT), Taiwan • **Guven Ciftci,** Faith University, Turkey • **Freddy Correa Montenegro,** Centro Colombo Americano, Cali, Colombia • **Alicia Craman de Carmand,** Idiomas Católica, Lima, Peru • **Jesús G. Díaz Osío,** Florida National College, Miami, USA • **Ruth Domínguez,** Universidad Central Bogotá, Colombia • **Roxana Echave,** El Cultural Arequipa, Peru • **Angélica Escobar Chávez,** Universidad de León, Mexico • **John Fieldeldy,** College of Engineering, Nihon University, Aizuwakamatsu-shi, Japan • **Herlinda Flores,** Centro de Idiomas Universidad Veracruzana, Mexico • **Claudia Franco,** Universidad Pedagógica Nacional, Colombia • **Andrea Fredricks,** Embassy CES, San Francisco, USA • **Chen-Chen Fu,** National Kaoshiung First Science Technology University, Taiwan • **María Irma Gallegos Peláez,** Universidad del Valle de México, Mexico City, Mexico • **Carolina García Carbajal,** El Cultural Arequipa, Peru • **Claudia Gavancho Terrazas,** ICPNA Cusco, Peru • **Adriana Gómez,** Centro Colombo Americano, Bogotá, Colombia • **Raphaël Goossens,** ICPNA Cusco, Peru • **Carlo Granados,** Universidad Central, Bogotá, Colombia • **Ralph Grayson,** Idiomas Católica, Lima, Peru • **Murat Gultekin,** Fatih University, Turkey • **Monika Hennessey,** ICPNA Chiclayo, Peru • **Lidia Hernández Medina,** Universidad del Valle de México, Mexico City, Mexico • **Jesse Huang,** National Central University, Taiwan • **Eric Charles Jones,** Seoul University of Technology, South Korea • **Jun-Chen Kuo,** Tajen University, Taiwan • **Susan Krieger,** Embassy CES, San Francisco, USA • **Robert Labelle,** Centre for Training and Development, Dawson College, Canada • **Erin Lemaistre,** Chung-Ang University, South Korea • **Eleanor S. Leu,** Soochow University, Taiwan • **Yihui Li (Stella Li),** Fooyin University, Taiwan • **Chin-Fan Lin,** Shih Hsin University, Taiwan • **Linda Lin,** Tatung Institute of Technology, Taiwan • **Kristen Lindblom,** Embassy CES, San Francisco, USA • **Ricardo López,** PROULEX, Guadalajara, Mexico • **Neil Macleod,** Kansai Gaidai University, Osaka, Japan • **Robyn McMurray,** Pusan National University, South Korea • **Paula Medina,** London Language Institute, Canada • **María Teresa Meléndez de Elorreaga,** ICPNA Chiclayo, Peru • **Sandra Cecilia Mora Espejo,** Universidad del Valle de México, Campus Tlalpan, Mexico City, Mexico • **Ricardo Nausa,** Centro Colombo Americano, Bogotá, Colombia • **Tim Newfields,** Tokyo University Faculty of Economics, Tokyo, Japan • **Mónica Nomberto,** ICPNA Chiclayo, Peru • **Scarlett Ostojic,** Idiomas Católica, Lima, Peru • **Ana Cristina Ochoa,** CCBEU Inter Americano, Curitiba, Brazil • **Doralba Pérez,** Universidad Pedagógica Nacional, Bogotá, Colombia • **David Perez Montalvo,** ICPNA Cusco, Peru • **Wahrena Elizabeth Pfeister,** University of Suwon, South Korea • **Wayne Allen Pfeister,** University of Suwon, South Korea • **Cecilia Ponce de León,** ICPNA Cusco, Peru • **Andrea Rebonato,** CCBEU Inter Americano, Curitiba, Brazil • **Elizabeth Rodríguez López,** El Cultural Trujillo, Peru • **Olga Rodríguez Romero,** El Cultural Trujillo, Peru • **Timothy Samuelson,** BridgeEnglish, Denver, USA • **Enrique Sánchez Guzmán,** PROULEX, Guadalajara, Mexico • **Letícia Santos,** ICBEU Ibiá, Brazil • **Lyndsay Shaeffer,** Embassy CES, San Francisco, USA • **John Eric Sherman,** Hong Ik University, South Korea • **João Vitor Soares,** NACC, São Paulo, Brazil • **Elena Sudakova,** English Language Center, Kiev, Ukraine • **Richard Swingle,** Kansai Gaidai College, Osaka, Japan • **Sandrine Ting,** St. John's University, Taiwan • **Shu-Ping Tsai,** Fooyin University, Taiwan • **José Luis Urbina Hurtado,** Universidad de León, Mexico • **Monica Urteaga,** Idiomas Católica, Lima, Peru • **Juan Carlos Villafuerte,** ICPNA Cusco, Peru • **Dr. Wen-hsien Yang,** National Kaohsiung Hospitality College, Kaohsiung, Taiwan • **Holger Zamora,** ICPNA Cusco, Peru.

Learning Objectives

Unit	Communication Goals	Vocabulary	Grammar
1 **Make Small Talk**	• Make small talk • Describe a busy schedule • Develop your cultural awareness • Discuss how culture changes over time	• Ways to ask about proper address • Intensifiers • Manners and etiquette	• Tag questions: usage, form, and common errors • The past perfect: meaning, form, and usage **GRAMMAR BOOSTER** • Tag questions: short answers • Verb usage: present and past (review)
2 **Health Matters**	• Call in sick • Make a medical or dental appointment • Discuss types of treatments • Talk about medications	• Dental emergencies • Symptoms • Medical procedures • Types of medical treatments • Medications	• Modal <u>must</u>: drawing conclusions • <u>Will be able to</u> • Modals <u>may</u> and <u>might</u> **GRAMMAR BOOSTER** • Other ways to draw conclusions: <u>probably</u>; <u>most likely</u>; common errors • Expressing possibility with <u>maybe</u>; common errors
3 **Getting Things Done**	• Get someone else to do something • Request express service • Evaluate the quality of service • Plan a meeting or social event	• Ways to help out another person • Ways to indicate acceptance • Services • Planning an event	• Causatives <u>get</u>, <u>have</u>, and <u>make</u> • The passive causative **GRAMMAR BOOSTER** • <u>Let</u> to indicate permission • Causative <u>have</u>: common errors • The passive causative: the <u>by</u> phrase
4 **Reading for Pleasure**	• Recommend a book • Offer to lend something • Describe your reading habits • Discuss the quality of reading materials	• Types of books • Ways to describe a book • Ways to enjoy reading	• Noun clauses: usage, form, and common errors • Noun clauses: embedded questions ◦ Form and common errors **GRAMMAR BOOSTER** • Verbs and adjectives that can be followed by clauses with <u>that</u> • Embedded questions: usage and common errors, punctuation, with infinitives • Noun clauses as subjects and objects

5 **Natural Disasters**	• Convey a message
	• Report news
	• Describe natural disasters
	• Prepare for an emergency
		• Severe weather and other natural disasters
		• Adjectives of severity
		• Emergency preparations and supplies
			• Indirect speech:
			  ◦ Imperatives
			  ◦ <u>Say</u> and <u>tell</u>
			  ◦ Tense changes
			GRAMMAR BOOSTER
			• Direct speech: punctuation rules
			• Indirect speech: optional tense changes
			  ◦ Form and common errors

Conversation Strategies	Listening / Pronunciation	Reading	Writing
• Talk about the weather to begin a conversation with someone you don't know • Use question tags to encourage someone to make small talk • Ask about how someone wants to be addressed • Answer a <u>Do you mind</u> question with <u>Absolutely not</u> to indicate agreement • Say <u>That was nothing</u> to indicate that something even more surprising happened • Use <u>Wow!</u> to indicate that you are impressed	**Listening Skills:** • Listen for main ideas • Listen to summarize • Confirm the correct paraphrases **Pronunciation:** • Rising and falling intonation of tag questions	**Texts:** • A business meeting memo and agenda • A magazine article about formal dinner etiquette of the past • A survey about culture change • A photo story **Skills/Strategies:** • Predict • Confirm facts • Summarize	**Task:** • Write a formal and an informal e-mail message **WRITING BOOSTER** • Formal e-mail etiquette
• Introduce disappointing information with <u>I'm afraid …</u> • Express disappointment with <u>I'm sorry to hear that</u> • Show concern with <u>Is something wrong?</u> and <u>That must be awful</u> • Begin a request for assistance with <u>I wonder if …</u> • Use <u>Let's see …</u> to indicate you are checking for something • Confirm an appointment with <u>I'll / We'll see you then</u> • Express emphatic thanks with <u>I really appreciate it</u>	**Listening Skills:** • Auditory discrimination • Listen for details **Pronunciation:** • Intonation of lists	**Texts:** • A travel tips website about dental emergencies • A brochure about choices in medical treatments • A patient information form • A medicine label • A photo story **Skills/Strategies:** • Understand from context • Relate to personal experience • Draw conclusions	**Task:** • Write an essay comparing two types of medical treatments **WRITING BOOSTER** • Comparisons and contrasts
• Use <u>I would, but …</u> and an excuse to politely turn down a request • Indicate acceptance of someone's excuse with <u>That's OK. I understand</u> • Suggest an alternative with <u>Maybe you could …</u> • Soften a request by beginning it with <u>Do you think you could …</u> • Soften an almost certain <u>no</u> with <u>That might be difficult</u> • Use <u>Well, …</u> to indicate willingness to reconsider	**Listening Skills:** • Listen for specific information • Listen for main ideas • Listen for order of details • Listen to summarize **Pronunciation:** • Emphatic stress to express enthusiasm	**Texts:** • A survey about procrastination • A travel article about tailoring services • A photo story **Skills/Strategies:** • Identify supporting details • Activate language from a text	**Task:** • Write an essay expressing a point of view about procrastination **WRITING BOOSTER** • Supporting an opinion with personal examples
• Use <u>Actually</u> to show appreciation for someone's interest in a topic • Soften a question with <u>Could you tell me …?</u> • Indicate disappointment with <u>Too bad</u> • Use <u>I'm dying to …</u> to indicate extreme interest • Say <u>That would be great</u> to express gratitude for someone's willingness to do something	**Listening Skills:** • Listen to take notes • Listen to infer a speaker's point of view and support your opinion **Pronunciation:** • Sentence stress in short answers with <u>so</u>	**Texts:** • An online bookstore website • Capsule descriptions of four best-sellers • A magazine article about comics • A photo story **Skills/Strategies:** • Recognize points of view • Critical thinking	**Task:** • Write a summary and review of something you've read **WRITING BOOSTER** • Summarizing
• Use <u>I would, but …</u> to politely turn down an offer • Say <u>Will do</u> to agree to a request for action • Use <u>Well</u> to begin providing requested information • Say <u>What a shame</u> to show empathy for a misfortune • Introduce reassuring contrasting information with <u>But, …</u> • Say <u>Thank goodness for that</u> to indicate relief	**Listening Skills:** • Listen for main ideas • Listen for details • Listen to paraphrase • Listen to infer meaning **Pronunciation:** • Direct and indirect speech: rhythm	**Texts:** • News headlines • A textbook article about earthquakes • Statistical charts • A photo story **Skills/Strategies:** • Paraphrase • Confirm facts • Identify cause and effect • Interpret data from a chart	**Task:** • Write a procedure for how to prepare for an emergency **WRITING BOOSTER** • Organizing detail statements by order of importance

CONTENTS

STUDENT BOOK

UNIT 1	Make Small Talk	2
UNIT 2	Health Matters	14
UNIT 3	Getting Things Done	26
UNIT 4	Reading for pleasure	38
UNIT 5	Natural Disasters	50

REFERENCE CHARTS

Grammar Booster 62

Writing Booster 70

Top Notch Pop Lyrics 75

WORKBOOK

UNIT 1	Make Small Talk	79
UNIT 2	Health Matters	89
UNIT 3	Getting Things Done	100
UNIT 4	Reading for pleasure	111
UNIT 5	Natural Disasters	122

To the Teacher

What is Top Notch?

Top Notch is a six-level* communicative course that prepares adults and young adults to interact successfully and confidently with both native and non-native speakers of English.

The goal of the Top Notch course is to make English unforgettable through:

- ► Multiple exposures to new language
- ► Numerous opportunities to practice it
- ► Deliberate and intensive recycling

The Top Notch course has two beginning levels: Top Notch Fundamentals for true beginners and Top Notch 1 for false beginners.

Each full level of Top Notch contains enough material for 60 to 90 hours of classroom instruction. A wide choice of supplementary components makes it easy to tailor Top Notch to the needs of your classes.

*Summit 1 and Summit 2 are the titles of the fifth and sixth levels of the Top Notch course. All Student's Books are available in split editions with bound-in workbooks.

The Top Notch instructional design

Daily confirmation of progress
Each easy-to-follow two-page lesson begins with a clearly stated communication goal. All lesson activities are integrated with the goal and systematically build toward a final speaking activity in which students demonstrate achievement of the goal. "Can-do" statements in each unit ensure students' awareness of the continuum of their progress.

A purposeful conversation syllabus
Memorable conversation models provide essential and practical social language that students can carry "in their pockets" for use in real life. Guided conversation pair work enables students to modify, personalize, and extend each model so they can use it to communicate their own thoughts and needs. Free discussion activities are carefully crafted so students can continually retrieve and use the language from the models. All conversation models are informed by the Longman Corpus of Spoken American English.

An emphasis on cultural fluency
Recognizing that English is a global language, Top Notch actively equips students to interact socially with people from a variety of cultures and deliberately prepares them to understand accented speakers from diverse language backgrounds.

Intensive vocabulary development
Students actively work with a rich vocabulary of high-frequency words, collocations, and expressions in all units of the Student's Book. Clear illustrations and definitions clarify meaning and provide support for independent study, review, and test preparation. Systematic recycling promotes smooth and continued acquisition of vocabulary from the beginning to the advanced levels of the course.

A dynamic approach to grammar
An explicit grammar syllabus is supported by charts containing clear grammar rules, relevant examples, and explanations of meaning and use. Numerous grammar exercises provide focused practice, and grammar usage is continually activated in communication exercises that illustrate the grammar being learned.

A dedicated pronunciation syllabus
Focused pronunciation, rhythm, and intonation practice is included in each unit, providing application of each pronunciation point to the target language of the unit and facilitating comprehensible pronunciation.

UNIT 1
Make small talk

Preview

GOALS After Unit 1, you will be able to:
1. Make small talk.
2. Describe a busy schedule.
3. Develop your cultural awareness.
4. Discuss how culture changes over time.

ROWAN PAPER International

Annual Meeting for Affiliates
Bangkok, Thailand
March 24 – 27

Meeting Etiquette

WELCOME TO OUR AFFILIATES FROM ALL PARTS OF THE WORLD!

Since we all come together from different traditions and cultures, here are some guidelines to make this meeting run smoothly:

- Please arrive promptly for meetings.

- Dress is business casual: no ties or jackets required. However, no denim or shorts, please. Ladies should feel free to wear slacks.

- Please refrain from making or taking calls during meetings. Put all cell phones and pagers on vibrate mode. If you have an urgent call, please step outside into the corridor.

- Note: Everyone is on a first-name basis.

FYI: Food is international style. All meals will provide non-meat options. If you have a special dietary requirement, please speak with Ms. Parnthep at the front desk.

ROWAN PAPER International

Agenda–March 24

Time	Event	Location
8:30:	Breakfast buffet in Salon Bangkok	Ballroom
9:15:	Welcome and opening remarks Philippe Martin President and CEO	Ballroom
9:45:	First quarter results and discussion Angela de Groot CFO	
10:30:	Coffee break	Ballroom
11:00:	International outlook and integrated marketing plans Sergio Montenegro	
11:00:	Regional marketing plans • U.S. and Canada Group • Mexico and Central America Group • Caribbean Group • South America (Southern Cone and Andes) Group • Brazil	Salon A Salon B Salon C Salon D Salon E

A Read and summarize the etiquette guidelines for an international business meeting. Write four statements beginning with <u>Don't</u>.

B Discussion Why do you think Rowan Paper International feels it's necessary to tell participants about meeting etiquette? What could happen if they didn't clarify expectations?

C 🔊 **Photo story** Read and listen to a conversation between two participants at the meeting in Bangkok.

ENGLISH FOR TODAY'S WORLD
connecting people from different cultures and language backgrounds

Teresa: Allow me to introduce myself. I am Teresa Segovia from the Santiago office. *Sawatdee-Kaa*.
Surat: Where did you learn the *wai**? You're Chilean, aren't you?
Teresa: Yes, I am. But I have a friend in Chile from Thailand.

Surat: Well, *Sawatdee-Khrab*. Nice to meet you, Ms. Segovia. I'm Surat Leekpai.
Teresa: No need to be so formal. Please call me Terri.
Surat: And please call me Surat.
Teresa: OK. Surat, do you mind my asking you a question about that, though?
Surat: Not at all.

Teresa: Is it customary in Thailand for people to be on a first-name basis?
Surat: Well, at company meetings in English, always. In other situations, though, people tend to be a little more formal. It's probably best to watch what others do. You know what they say: "When in Rome, . . ."
Teresa: Mm-hmm . . ., "do as the Romans do!"

Teresa: Spanish speaker / Surat: Thai speaker
*Thais greet each other with a gesture called the <u>wai</u> and by saying "Sawatdee-Kaa" (women) / "Sawatdee-Khrab" (men).

D Think and explain Answer the following questions.

1 Why was Surat surprised about the way Teresa greeted him? How do you know he was surprised?
2 Why do you think Teresa decided to say "Sawatdee-Kaa"?
3 What did Teresa mean when she said, "No need to be so formal"?
4 What do you think the difference is between "People *tend to be* a little more formal" and "People *are* a little more formal"?
5 What do you think the saying "When in Rome, do as the Romans do" means?

E Personalization Look at the chart. If you took a trip to another country, how would you like to be addressed? Explain your reasons.

I'd like to be called . . .	Always	In some situations	Never
by my title and my family name.	☐	☐	☐
by my first name.	☐	☐	☐
by my nickname.	☐	☐	☐
I'd prefer to follow the local customs.	☐	☐	☐
Other	☐	☐	☐

F Discussion Talk about the following questions.

1 In your opinion, is it inappropriate for two people of very different status (such as a CEO and an assistant) to be on a first-name basis? Explain.
2 In general, when do you think people should use first names with each other? When should they use titles and last names? Explain your reasons.

LESSON 1

GOAL Make small talk

CONVERSATION MODEL

A 🔊 Read and listen to two people meeting and making small talk.

A: Good morning. Beautiful day, isn't it?
B: It really is. By the way, I'm Kazuko Toshinaga.
A: I'm Jane Quitt. Nice to meet you.
B: Nice to meet you, too.
A: Do you mind if I call you Kazuko?
B: Absolutely not. Please do.
A: And please call me Jane.

Ways to ask about proper address
Do you mind if I call you [Kazuko]?
Would it be rude to call you [Kazuko]?
What would you like to be called?
How do you prefer to be addressed?
Do you use Ms. or Mrs.?

B 🔊 **Rhythm and intonation** Listen again and repeat. Then practice the Conversation Model with a partner.

GRAMMAR Tag questions: use and form

Use tag questions to confirm information you already think is true or to encourage someone to make small talk with you.
 (It's a) beautiful day, **isn't it**?

When the statement is affirmative, the tag is negative. When the statement is negative, the tag is affirmative.

Be careful!
Use aren't I? for negative tag questions after I am.
 I'm on time, **aren't I**? BUT I'm not late, **am I**?
Use pronouns, not names or other nouns, in tag questions.
 Bangkok is in Thailand, **isn't it**?
 NOT isn't Bangkok?

affirmative		negative	
You're Lee,	aren't you?	You're not Amy,	are you?
She speaks Thai,	doesn't she?	I don't know you,	do I?
He's going to drive,	isn't he?	We're not going to eat here,	are we?
They'll be here later,	won't they?	It won't be long,	will it?
You were there,	weren't you?	He wasn't driving,	was he?
They left,	didn't they?	We didn't know,	did we?
It's been a great day,	hasn't it?	She hasn't been here long,	has she?
Ann would like Quito,	wouldn't she?	You wouldn't do that,	would you?
They can hear me,	can't they?	He can't speak Japanese,	can he?

GRAMMAR BOOSTER ▸ p. 122
• Tag questions: short answers

A Find the grammar Find a tag question in the Photo Story on page 3.

B Grammar practice Complete each statement with a tag question.

1 Rob is your manager, ...?
2 I turned off the projector, ...?
3 Tim is going to present next, ...?
4 She won't be at the meeting before 2:00, ...?
5 We haven't forgotten anything, ...?
6 There was no one here from China, ...?
7 The agenda can't be printed in the business center before 8:00 A.M., ...?
8 They were explaining the etiquette rules, ...?
9 She wants to be addressed by her first name, ...?
10 It was a great day, ...?

PRONUNCIATION Rising and falling intonation of tag questions

A 🔊 Rising intonation usually indicates that the speaker is confirming the correctness of information. Read and listen. Then listen again and repeat.

1 People use first names here, don't they?
2 That meeting was great, wasn't it?
3 It's a beautiful day for a walk, isn't it?

B 🔊 Falling intonation usually indicates that the speaker expects the listener to agree. Read and listen. Then listen again and repeat.

1 People use first names here, don't they?
2 That meeting was great, wasn't it?
3 It's a beautiful day for a walk, isn't it?

C Pair work Take turns reading the examples of tag questions in the grammar chart on page 4. Read each with both rising and falling intonation.

NOW YOU CAN Make small talk

A Pair work Change the Conversation Model to greet a classmate. Make small talk. Ask each other about how you would like to be addressed. Then change partners.

A: Good ...., ..., isn't it?
B: It really is. By the way, I'm ....
A: I'm ....

Don't stop!
• Continue making small talk.
• Get to know your new classmates.
• Ask about families, jobs, travel, etc.

Ideas for tag questions
• [Awful] weather, ...
• Nice [afternoon], ...
• Great [English class], ...
• [Good] food, ...
• The food is [terrible], ...

B Extension Write your name and a few facts about yourself on a sheet of paper and put it on a table. Choose another classmate's paper, read it quickly, and put it back on the table. Then meet that person and confirm the information you read, using tag questions.

Maria Carbone
I grew up here, but my parents are from Italy. I started studying English when I was in primary school.

"Maria, hi! I'm Deborah. Your parents are from Italy, aren't they?"

LESSON 2

GOAL Describe a busy schedule

GRAMMAR The past perfect: meaning, form, and use

Use the past perfect to describe an action that happened (or didn't happen) before another action or before a specific time in the past.
   Our flight **had arrived** by noon.
   The meeting **hadn't** yet **begun** when we arrived.

Past perfect form: had + past participle

Use the past perfect with the simple past tense to clarify which of two past events occurred first.
   The meeting **had ended** late, so we had a short lunch.
      (First action: The meeting ended; later action: we had lunch.)
   When the tour **started**, Ann **had** already **met** Kazuko.
      (First action: Ann and Kazuko met; later action: the tour started.)

Note: In informal speech, it's common to use the simple past tense instead of the past perfect. The words <u>by</u>, <u>before</u>, and <u>after</u> often clarify the order of the events.
   By April, he **started** his new job.
   Before I got married, I **got** a degree in marketing.
   After I learned to make presentations, they **promoted** me.

GRAMMAR BOOSTER ▸ p. 123
• Verb usage: present and past (review)

A Grammar practice Choose the correct meaning for each statement.

1 "Before they decided to have the meeting in Bangkok, I had already decided to take my vacation there."
   ☐ First they decided to have the meeting in Bangkok. Then I decided to take my vacation there.
   ☐ First I decided to take my vacation in Bangkok. Then they decided to have the meeting there.

2 "By the time she got to the meeting, she had already reviewed the agenda."
   ☐ First she reviewed the agenda. Then she got to the meeting.
   ☐ First she got to the meeting. Then she reviewed the agenda.

3 "They had already asked us to turn off our cell phones when the CEO began her presentation."
   ☐ First they asked us to turn off our cell phones. Then the CEO began her presentation.
   ☐ First the CEO began her presentation. Then they asked us to turn off our cell phones.

4 "I had changed into business casual dress before the meeting started."
   ☐ First the meeting started. Then I changed into business casual dress.
   ☐ First I changed into business casual dress. Then the meeting started.

B Meg Ash has to travel to a sales meeting in Seoul tomorrow. It's now 7:00 P.M. Read her to-do list and complete the statements, using <u>already</u> or <u>yet</u>.

1 At 8:30 Meg .... her laundry, but she .... the cat to her mom's house.

2 By 10:45 she .... the cat to her mom's house, but she .... for the meeting.

3 By 12:15 she .... the sales binders at Office Plus, but she .... lunch with Adam.

4 At 1:30 she .... lunch with Adam, but she .... the DVDs to FilmPix.

5 By 2:15 she .... the DVDs to FilmPix, but she .... the dentist.

6 At 5:55 she .... the dentist, but she .... a manicure.

Monday, January 4

8:00	Drop off the laundry at Minute Wash.
9:00	
10:00	Take the cat to Mom's house.
11:00	Pack for the meeting.
12:00	Pick up the sales binders at Office Plus.
1:00	Lunch with Adam
2:00	Return the DVDs to FilmPix.
3:00	
4:00	See dentist. ☹
5:00	5:30 Pick up the laundry from Minute Wash.
6:00	Get a manicure if there's time!
7:00	
8:00	

CONVERSATION MODEL

A 🔊 Read and listen to someone describing a busy schedule.

A: So how was your day?
B: Unbelievably busy. By 9:00 I had already taken the placement test, registered for class, and bought my books.
A: That's a lot to do before 9:00!
B: That was nothing. At 10:00 I had to be across town for a meeting.
A: Wow!
B: And then I had to get back for the class at 1:00.
A: What did you do about lunch?
B: Well, when I got to class, I hadn't eaten yet, so I just got a snack.
A: You must be pretty hungry by now!

🔊 **Intensifiers**
+++ unbelievably
+++ incredibly
++ really
++ so
+ pretty

B 🔊 **Rhythm and intonation** Listen again and repeat. Then practice the Conversation Model with a partner.

NOW YOU CAN Describe a busy schedule

A Pair work Change the Conversation Model to describe a busy day, morning, afternoon, evening, week, or any other period of time in the past. Then change roles.

A: So how was your ....?
B: .... busy. By .... I .... already ....
A: That's a lot to do before ....!
B: That was nothing. ....
A: Wow!
B: And then I ....
A: What did you do about ....?
B: ....
A: You must be ....!

Don't stop!
• Ask more questions about your partner's activities.
• Provide more details about the activities.

B Change partners Practice the conversation again. Ask other classmates to describe their busy schedules.

LESSON 3

GOAL Develop your cultural awareness

BEFORE YOU LISTEN

A 🔊 **Vocabulary** • *Manners and etiquette* Read and listen. Then listen again and repeat.

etiquette the "rules" for polite behavior in society or in a particular group

cultural literacy knowing about and respecting the culture of others

table manners rules for polite behavior when eating with other people

punctuality the habit of being on time

impolite not polite, rude

offensive extremely rude or impolite

customary usual or traditional in a particular culture

taboo not allowed because of very strong cultural or religious rules

B Complete each sentence with the correct word or phrase from the Vocabulary.

1 It's (taboo / impolite) to eat pork in some religions. No one would ever do it.
2 Many people believe that (cultural literacy / punctuality) is important and that being late is impolite.
3 In some cultures, it's (offensive / customary) to take pictures of people without permission, so few people do that.
4 Some people think that talking with a mouth full of food is an example of bad (cultural literacy / table manners).
5 In some cultures, it's (customary / offensive) to name children after a living relative, and most people observe that tradition.
6 Each culture has rules of (cultural literacy / etiquette) that are important for visitors to that country to know.
7 In more conservative cultures, it's slightly (impolite / taboo) to call someone by his or her first name without being invited, but it isn't truly offensive.
8 The most successful global travelers today have developed their (punctuality / cultural literacy) so they are aware of differences in etiquette from culture to culture.

C Discussion Discuss your opinions, using the Vocabulary.

1 What are some good ways to teach children etiquette? Give examples.
2 Do you know of any differences in etiquette between your culture and others? Give examples.
3 Why are table manners important in almost all cultures? How would people behave if there were no rules?

Some people eat with a fork, some with chopsticks, and some with their hands.

LISTENING COMPREHENSION

A 🔊 **Listen for main ideas** Look at the subjects on the chart. Listen to three calls from a radio show. Check the subjects that are discussed during each call.

B 🔊 **Summarize** Listen again. On a separate sheet of paper, take notes about the calls. Then, with a partner, write a summary of each call. Use the Vocabulary.

Subjects	1 Arturo / Jettrin	2 Hiroko / Nadia	3 Javier / Sujeet
table manners	☐	☐	☐
greetings	☐	☐	☐
dress and clothing	☐	☐	☐
male / female behavior	☐	☐	☐
taboos	☐	☐	☐
offensive behavior	☐	☐	☐
punctuality	☐	☐	☐
language	☐	☐	☐

NOW YOU CAN Develop your cultural awareness

A Frame your ideas With a partner, look at the questions about your culture on the notepad. Discuss each question and write your answers to the questions.

- How do people greet each other when they meet for the first time?
- How do they greet each other when they already know each other?
- Are greeting customs different for men and women? How?
- When and how do you address people formally?
- When and how do you address people informally?
- What are some do's and don'ts for table manners?
- Are certain foods or beverages taboo?
- What are some taboo conversation topics?
- What are the customs about punctuality?
- What is a customary gift if you are visiting someone's home?
- Are there any gift taboos (kinds of flowers, etc.)?
- Are there places where certain clothes would be inappropriate?
- Is there an important aspect of your culture that's not on this list?

C Group work Role-play a conversation with a visitor to your country. Tell the visitor about your culture. Use the answers to the questions on the notepad.

❝ It's bad table manners to pick up a soup bowl and drink soup from it. You have to use a spoon. ❞

❝ It's not customary for a man to extend his hand to shake hands with a woman. He should wait for the woman to do that. ❞

B Discussion Combine classmates' notes on the board for the class to share. Does everyone agree? Discuss your differences of opinion.

LESSON 4

GOAL: Discuss how culture changes over time

BEFORE YOU READ

A Use prior knowledge In what ways do you think table manners have changed since the days when your grandparents were children?

B Predict the topic Look at the title of the article, the original date of publication, and the internal headings. Use those cues to predict what the article will be about.

READING 1:14

Formal Dinner Etiquette

It is very discourteous for a guest to be late. Arrive at least five minutes before the hour set for the dinner. If for some unavoidable reason you cannot arrive on time, telephone the hostess and explain the reason to her. Etiquette only requires that she wait for fifteen minutes before beginning the meal. If it has been impossible for you to notify her and she has started the meal, go to her, offer apologies, and take your place at the table as quickly as possible.

SEATING
The hostess leads the female guests into the dining room. The host and the male guests follow. The hostess then tells her guests where to sit. She must always have the seating arrangement planned in advance in order to avoid confusion and delay.

Each person stands casually behind his chair until the hostess starts to take her seat. The man helps his dinner partner to be seated and also helps move her chair as she rises. Each person moves to the left of the chair to be seated and also rises from the left.

Originally published in 1940 in the United States

THE MEAL
At a small dinner party, do not start to eat until all guests are served. At a large dinner party, you may start to eat as soon as those near you have been served. Do not eat too fast. Do not talk while you have food in your mouth, and keep the mouth closed while you chew your food. Elbows should not be put on the table when you are eating (however, between courses at a restaurant, if you cannot hear your companion, it is permissible to lean forward on your elbows).

If silver is dropped on the floor, leave it there. If an accident happens at the table, apologize briefly to your hostess.

The hostess continues to eat as long as her guests do. When all have finished, she rises from the table and the others follow.

DEPARTING
If you have no dinner partner, push your chair from the table by taking hold of each side of the seat of the chair. Don't rest your hands or arms on the table to push yourself up.

It is not necessary to remain longer than thirty minutes after a dinner if the invitation does not include the entire evening. However, one should avoid appearing in a hurry to leave.

Source: www.Oldandsold.com

A Confirm facts On a separate sheet of paper, answer the questions about dinner party etiquette in the 1940s.

1. If the dinner party invitation is for 8:00, what time should guests arrive?

   Guests should arrive by 7:55 at the latest.

2. If a guest is going to be late, what should he or she do?
3. Who decides where guests should sit at the table?
4. What are the different roles or expectations of men and women at a dinner party?
5. When should a guest begin eating?
6. What should a guest do if a fork or a knife falls to the floor?
7. What should a guest do if he or she spills a drink on the table?
8. How long should the host or hostess continue eating?
9. What should a guest do when the host or hostess leaves the table?
10. How long should guests stay after dinner is over?

B Summarize Summarize how dinner party etiquette has changed since the 1940s. Use the questions in Exercise A on page 10 as a guide.

On your *ActiveBook* Self-Study Disc:
Extra Reading Comprehension Questions

NOW YOU CAN   Discuss how culture changes over time

A Frame your ideas Think about how culture has changed since your grandparents were your age. Complete the survey.

Culture Survey

	have changed a little	have changed a lot	Is the change for the better? (YES or NO)	
1. Table manners	☐	☐	☐	☐
2. Musical tastes	☐	☐	☐	☐
3. Dating customs	☐	☐	☐	☐
4. Clothing customs	☐	☐	☐	☐
5. Rules about formal behavior	☐	☐	☐	☐
6. Rules about punctuality	☐	☐	☐	☐
7. Forms of address	☐	☐	☐	☐
8. Male / female roles in the workplace	☐	☐	☐	☐
9. Male / female roles in the home	☐	☐	☐	☐

Total YES answers: _____

Are you a dinosaur or a chameleon?

How many times did you check YES in the third column?

0–3 = Definitely a dinosaur. You prefer to stick with tradition. Your motto: "If it isn't broken, don't fix it!"

4–6 = A little of both. You're willing to adapt to change, but not too fast. Your motto: "Easy does it!"

7–9 = Definitely a chameleon. You adapt to change easily. Your motto: "Out with the old, in with the new!"

B Pair work Compare and discuss your answers. Provide specific examples of changes for each answer. Use the past perfect if you can.

C Discussion Talk about how culture has changed. Include these topics in your discussion:

* Which changes do you think are good? Which changes are not good? Explain your reasons.
* How do you think older people feel about these changes?
* Do you think men and women differ in their feelings about cultural change? If so, how?

> "I think clothing customs have become less modest. My mother had to wear a uniform to school. But by the time I started school, girls had stopped wearing them. Now girls can go to school in jeans and even shorts!"

Be sure to recycle this language.

Formality
be on a first-name basis
prefer to be addressed by ___
It's impolite to ___ .
It's offensive to ___ .
It's customary to ___ .
It isn't customary to ___ .

Tag questions
[People don't ___ as much], do they?
[Customs used to be ___], didn't they?

Agreement / Disagreement
I agree.
I think you're right.
I disagree.
Actually, I don't agree because ___ .
Really? I think ___ .

Review

A 🔊 **Listening comprehension** Listen to the conversations between people introducing themselves. Check the statement that correctly paraphrases the main idea.

1. ☐ She'd like to be addressed by her title and family name.
   ☐ She'd like to be addressed by her first name.
2. ☐ She'd prefer to be called by her first name.
   ☐ She'd prefer to be called by her title and last name.
3. ☐ It's customary to call people by their first name there.
   ☐ It's not customary to call people by their first name there.
4. ☐ He's comfortable with the policy about names.
   ☐ He's not comfortable with the policy about names.
5. ☐ She prefers to use the title "Mrs."
   ☐ She prefers to use the title "Dr."

> 1:16 / 1:17
> **Top Notch Pop**
> "It's a Great Day for Love"
> Lyrics p. 149

B Complete each sentence with a tag question.

1. You're not from around here, ...?
2. You were in this class last year, ...?
3. They haven't been here since yesterday, ...?
4. Before the class, she hadn't yet told them how she wanted to be addressed, ...?
5. I can bring flowers as a gift for the hosts, ...?
6. You won't be back in time for dinner, ...?
7. I met you on the tour in Nepal, ...?
8. We'll have a chance to discuss this tomorrow, ...?
9. They were going to dinner, ...?
10. My friends are going to be surprised to see you, ...?

C Complete each statement with the correct word or phrase.

1. Offending other people when eating a meal is an example of bad ....
2. Each country has customs and traditions about how to behave in social situations. The rules are sometimes called ....
3. Each culture has its own sense of .... It's important to understand people's ideas about lateness.

D Writing On a separate sheet of paper, write two e-mail messages—one formal and one informal—telling someone about the cultural traditions in your country. Review the questionnaire about cultural traditions on page 9 for information to select from.

- For the formal e-mail, imagine you are writing to a businessperson who is coming to your country on a business trip.
- For the informal e-mail, imagine you are writing to a friend who is visiting your country as a tourist.

WRITING BOOSTER ▸ p. 141
- Formal e-mail etiquette
- Guidance for Exercise D

ORAL REVIEW

Tell a story First, look at the pictures and tell the story of the Garzas and the Itos on June 10. Then, look at the itineraries below and use the past perfect to talk about what they had done by June 5. Start like this:

By June 5, the Itos had been to . . .

Pair work Create conversations.
1 Create a conversation for the two men in the first picture. Each man tells the other how he'd like to be addressed.
2 Create a conversation for the two women in the second picture. The women are making small talk.
3 Create a conversation for the people in the third picture. Ask and answer questions about the their trips to Peru. Use the past perfect when possible.

June 10, 10:00 A.M.

María and Antonio Garza

Haru and Kimi Ito

Later that day

GLOBAL ADVENTURES, INC.

Haru and Kimi Ito—Peru Itinerary

May 29
Lima: María Angola Hotel
La Paz 610, Miraflores

May 31
Puno: Casa Andina Classic
Jr. Independencia 185, Plaza de Armas

June 4
Cusco: Novotel
San Agustín 239

June 9
Machu Picchu: Hanaq Pacha Hotel
(Aguas Calientes)

GetAway Travel, Inc.

María and Antonio Garza— Peru itinerary

May 30
Lima: María Angola Hotel
La Paz 610, Miraflores

June 3
Arequipa: Tierra Sur Hotel
Consuelo 210

June 6
Nasca: Brabant Hostel
Calle Juan Matta 978

June 9
Machu Picchu: Hanaq Pacha Hotel
(Aguas Calientes)

NOW I CAN...

☐ Make small talk.
☐ Describe a busy schedule.
☐ Develop cultural awareness.
☐ Discuss how culture changes over time.

UNIT 2

Health Matters

Preview

GOALS After Unit 2, you will be able to:
1. Call in sick.
2. Make a medical or dental appointment.
3. Discuss types of treatments.
4. Talk about medications.

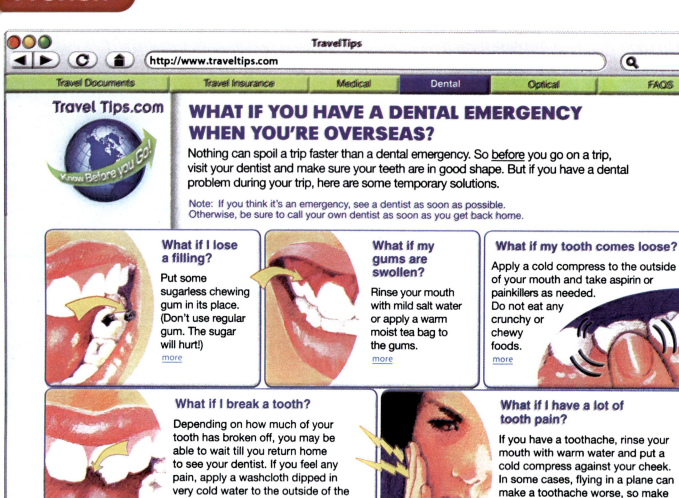

Information source: www.webmd.com

A Discussion Do you think the information in the website is useful? Why do you think some people would wait until they got back home to see a dentist?

B Pair work Discuss each of the situations described in the website and what you would do. Circle yes or no.

I would . . .
- ignore the problem.   yes   no
- make an appointment to see a dentist right away.   yes   no
- call or e-mail my own dentist and ask for advice.   yes   no
- use the remedy suggested in the website.   yes   no
- use my own remedy (explain).   yes   no

C 🔊 **Photo story** Read and listen to someone with a dental emergency during a trip.

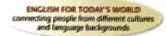
ENGLISH FOR TODAY'S WORLD
connecting people from different cultures and language backgrounds

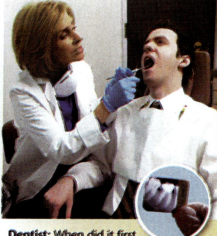

Guest: I need to see a dentist as soon as possible. I think it's an emergency. I was wondering if you might be able to recommend someone who speaks English.
Clerk: Let me check. Actually, there is one not far from here. Would you like me to make an appointment for you?
Guest: If you could. Thanks. I'm in a lot of pain.

Dentist: So I hear you're from overseas.
Patient: From Ecuador. Thanks for fitting me in.
Dentist: Luckily, I had a cancellation. So what brings you in today?
Patient: Well, this tooth is killing me.

Dentist: When did it first begin to hurt?
Patient: It's been bothering me since last night.
Dentist: Let's have a look. Open wide.
Patient: Ah . . .
Dentist: Well, let's take an X-ray and see what's going on.

Guest (Patient): Spanish speaker / Clerk and dentist: Russian speakers

D Focus on language Find the underlined statements in the Photo Story. Then use the context to help you restate each one in your own words.

1 I was wondering if you might be able to recommend someone who speaks English.
2 If you could. Thanks.
3 Thanks for fitting me in.
4 This tooth is killing me.
5 It's been bothering me since last night.
6 Let's have a look.
7 Let's take an X-ray and see what's going on.

E Personalize Have you—or has someone you know—ever had an emergency that required dental or medical attention? Complete the chart.

Where did it happen?	When did it happen?	What happened?

F Group work Tell your classmates about your emergency.

> "Last year, I went skiing and I broke my arm. I had to go to the emergency room at the hospital."

LESSON 1

GOAL: Call in sick

VOCABULARY — Symptoms

A 🔊 1:19 Read and listen. Then listen again and repeat.

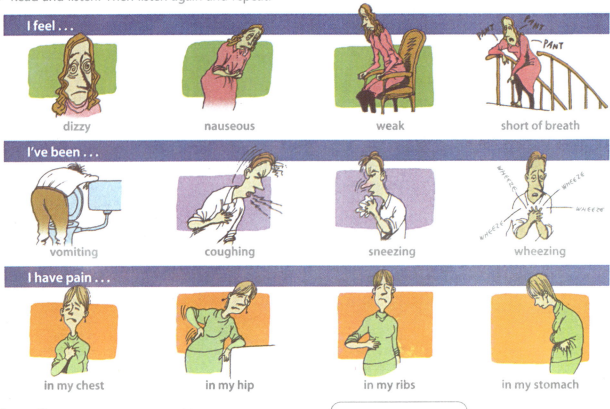

I feel... dizzy, nauseous, weak, short of breath

I've been... vomiting, coughing, sneezing, wheezing

I have pain... in my chest, in my hip, in my ribs, in my stomach

B Pair work Discuss what you would suggest to someone with some of the symptoms in the Vocabulary.

> "If you feel dizzy, you should lie down."

C 🔊 1:20 **Listening comprehension** Listen and check the symptoms each patient describes. Then listen again. If the patient has pain, write where it is.

	dizziness	nausea	weakness	vomiting	coughing	sneezing	wheezing	pain	If pain, where?
1	☐	☐	☐	☐	☐	☐	☐	☐	
2	☐	☐	☐	☐	☐	☐	☐	☐	
3	☐	☐	☐	☐	☐	☐	☐	☐	
4	☐	☐	☐	☐	☐	☐	☐	☐	
5	☐	☐	☐	☐	☐	☐	☐	☐	
6	☐	☐	☐	☐	☐	☐	☐	☐	

PRONUNCIATION — Intonation of lists

A 🔊 1:21 Use rising intonation on each item before the last item in a list. Use falling intonation on the last item. Read and listen. Then listen again and repeat.

1 I feel weak and dizzy.
2 I've been sneezing, coughing, and wheezing.
3 I have pain in my neck, my shoulders, my back, and my hip.

B Pair work Take turns using the Vocabulary to make lists of symptoms. Practice correct intonation for lists.

> " I feel dizzy, weak, and short of breath. "

GRAMMAR Modal *must*: drawing conclusions

Use must and the base form of a verb to indicate that you think something is probably true.
A: I think I just broke my tooth!
B: Oh, no. That **must** hurt.

A: The doctor said I should come in next week.
B: Oh, good. It **must not** be an emergency.

GRAMMAR BOOSTER ▸ p. 124
• Other ways to draw conclusions: *probably*; *most likely*

Grammar practice Complete the conversations by drawing conclusions, using *must* or *must not*.

1. A: You look awful! You .... (be) in a lot of pain.
   B: I am.

2. A: Gary just called. He has a bad headache.
   B: Too bad. He .... (want) to go running.

3. A: My doctor says I'm in perfect health.
   B: That's great. You .... (feel) really good.

4. A: Did you call the dentist?
   B: Yes, I did. But no one's answering. She .... (be) in today.

CONVERSATION MODEL

A 🔊 1:22 Read and listen to someone calling in sick.

A: I'm afraid I'm not going to be able to come in today.
B: I'm sorry to hear that. Is something wrong?
A: Actually, I'm not feeling too well. I've been coughing and wheezing for a couple of days.
B: That must be awful. Maybe you should see a doctor.
A: I think I will.
B: Good. Call me tomorrow and let me know how you feel. OK?

B 🔊 1:23 **Rhythm and intonation** Listen again and repeat. Then practice the Conversation Model with a partner.

NOW YOU CAN Call in sick

A Pair work Change the Conversation Model to describe other symptoms. Use *must* or *must not* to draw conclusions. Then change roles.

A: I'm afraid I'm not going to be able to .... today.
B: .... Is something wrong?
A: Actually, I'm not feeling too well. I ....
B: That must be .... Maybe you should ....
A: ....
B: .... Call me tomorrow and let me know how you feel, OK?

Don't stop!
• Ask more questions about your partner's symptoms.
• Give your partner more suggestions about what to do.

♻ **Be sure to recycle this language.**

Ask questions
Are you [coughing]?
Did you try ___?
Make suggestions
You should / You'd better ___.
Why don't you try ___?
How about ___?
Draw conclusions
You must feel awful / terrible.
That must hurt.

B Change partners Call in sick for other situations such as school or social events.

LESSON 2

GOAL Make a medical or dental appointment

GRAMMAR Will be able to; Modals may and might

Will be able to + base form: future ability
The doctor will be able to see you tomorrow. (= The doctor can see you tomorrow.)
She'll be able to play tennis again in a week or so. (= She can play tennis again in a week or so.)

May or might + base form: possibility
The dentist might have some time to see you this afternoon.
You may need to come in right away.

Note: You can use be able to with may and might for possibility or with must for drawing conclusions.

The doctor	may be able to	see you today.
I	might not be able to	get there till 6:00.
We	must be able to	park here—see the sign?
They	must not be able to	cancel the appointment.

GRAMMAR BOOSTER • p. 125
• Expressing possibility with *maybe*

Grammar practice Complete each conversation. Use *might*, *be able to*, *might be able to*, or *must not be able to* and the base form.

1 A: I'd like to see a dentist right away. I think it's an emergency.
B: Well, I .... you an appointment at 2:00. Would that be OK?
        get

2 A: Is Dr. Lindt in this morning? I'm not feeling very well.
B: She is, but she doesn't have any openings. However, she .... time to see you this afternoon.
        have

3 A: I think I .... allergic to strawberries. I had some for breakfast, and I have a rash all over my body.
        be
B: Then you'd better come in this morning. I .... you in right before noon.
        fit

4 A: I've been calling Mr. Reis for an hour. I know he's home, but no one's answering.
B: That's strange. He .... the phone.
        hear

VOCABULARY Medical procedures

A 🔊 1:24 Read and listen. Then listen again and repeat.

 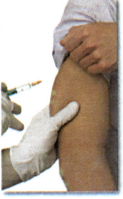 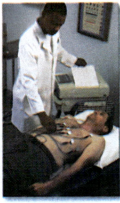 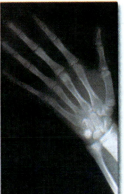 

a checkup / an examination   a shot / an injection   an EKG / an electrocardiogram   an X-ray   a blood test

B Pair work Discuss when a person might need each medical procedure from the Vocabulary.

> " If you have pain in your arm, you might need an X-ray. "

CONVERSATION MODEL

A 🔊 Read and listen to someone making an appointment.

A: Hello. Doctor Star's office. Can I help you?
B: Hello. I need to make an appointment for a blood test. I wonder if I might be able to come in early next week.
A: Let's see if I can fit you in. How about Tuesday?
B: Could I come in the morning?
A: Let me check . . . Would you be able to be here at 10:00?
B: That would be perfect.
A: We'll see you then.
B: Thanks! I really appreciate it.

B 🔊 **Rhythm and intonation** Listen again and repeat. Then practice the Conversation Model with a partner.

NOW YOU CAN Make a medical or dental appointment

A Pair work Make an appointment to see a doctor or dentist. Suggest a day. Write the appointment on the schedule. Then change roles.

A: Hello. Doctor .... 's office. Can I help you?
B: Hello. I need to make an appointment for .... I wonder if I might be able to come in ....
A: Let's see if I can fit you in. Would you be able to be here at .... ?
B: ....

Don't stop!
• Say you can't be there today.
• Discuss other days and times.

Ideas
• tomorrow
• next week
• early next week
• at the end of next week
• the week of [the 3rd]

B Change partners Make another appointment.

	Patient's name	Medical procedure
8:00	Bill Reed	blood test
9:00	Marie Petton	chest X-ray
10:00		
11:00		
12:00		
1:00	Angela Baker	checkup
2:00	Victor Gaines	flu shot
3:00		
4:00	Teresa Keyes	EKG
5:00		
6:00	Anna Holmes	chest X-ray
7:00		
8:00		
9:00		
10:00		

LESSON 3

GOAL Discuss types of treatments

BEFORE YOU READ

Warm-up What do you do when you get sick or you're in pain? Do you treat the problem yourself or see a doctor right away?

READING

Consider the choices...

CONVENTIONAL MEDICINE

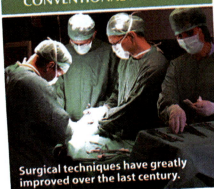

Surgical techniques have greatly improved over the last century.

The beginnings of conventional medicine can be traced back to the fifth century B.C.E. in ancient Greece. It is based on the scientific study of the human body and illness.

In the last century, there has been great progress in what doctors have been able to do with modern surgery and new medications. These scientific advances have made conventional medicine the method many people choose first when they need medical treatment.

HOMEOPATHY

Homeopathic remedies are popular in many countries.

Homeopathy was founded in the late eighteenth century in Germany. It is a low-cost system of natural medicine used by hundreds of millions of people worldwide.

In homeopathy, a patient's symptoms are treated with remedies that cause similar symptoms. The remedy is taken in very diluted form: 1 part remedy to one trillion (1,000,000,000,000) parts water.

HERBAL THERAPY

Herbs are used to treat many ailments.

Herbal medicine, often taken as teas or pills, has been practiced for thousands of years in almost all cultures around the world. In fact, many conventional medicines were discovered by scientists studying traditional uses of herbs for medical purposes.

The World Health Organization claims that 80% of the world's population uses some form of herbal therapy for their regular health care.

ACUPUNCTURE

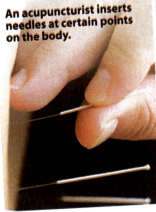

An acupuncturist inserts needles at certain points on the body.

Acupuncture originated in China over 5,000 years ago. Today, it is used worldwide for a variety of problems.

Acupuncture needles are inserted at certain points on the body to relieve pain and/or restore health. Many believe acupuncture may be effective in helping people stop smoking as well.

SPIRITUAL HEALING

Many believe meditation or prayer may help heal disease.

Also known as faith healing, or "mind and body connection," various forms of spiritual healing exist around the world. This is a form of healing that uses the mind or religious faith to treat illness.

A number of conventional doctors say that when they have not been able to help a patient, spiritual healing just may work.

Sources: www.alternativemedicine.com and www.holisticmed.com

UNIT 2

A Understand from context Five of these words have similar meanings. Cross out the three words that don't belong. Look at the article again for help.

remedy	treatment	therapy	advances
resources	healing	care	purposes

B Relate to personal experience Talk about the following questions.

1 Which of the treatments in the Reading have you or your family tried?
2 Which treatments do you think are the most effective? Why?

C Draw conclusions Decide which treatment or treatments each patient would probably NOT want to try and which he or she might prefer. Explain your answers, using <u>might</u> or <u>might not</u>. (More than one therapy might be appropriate.)

1 ❝I definitely want to see a doctor when I have a problem. But I want to avoid taking any strong medications or having surgery.❞

2 ❝I believe you have to heal yourself. You can't just expect a doctor to do everything for you.❞

3 ❝I think it would be crazy to try a health care method that isn't strongly supported by scientific research.❞

On your *ActiveBook* Self-Study Disc:
Extra Reading Comprehension Questions

NOW YOU CAN Discuss types of treatments

A Notepadding With a partner, discuss treatments you would choose for each ailment. What kind of practitioner would you visit? Complete your notepad.

Practitioners
- a conventional doctor
- a homeopathic doctor
- an acupuncturist
- an herbal therapist
- a spiritual healer

Ailment	You	Your partner
a cold		
a headache		
nausea		
back pain		
a high fever		
a broken finger		

B Discussion Compare the kinds of treatments you and your classmates would use. Say what you learned about your partner.

❝I would never try herbal therapy. I just don't think it works. My partner agrees.❞

❝My partner has been to an acupuncturist a number of times. It really helped with her back pain.❞

❝I see a homeopathic doctor regularly, but my partner doesn't believe in that. He prefers a conventional doctor.❞

LESSON 4

GOAL Talk about medications

BEFORE YOU LISTEN

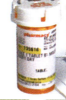

Medicine label information
Dosage: Take 1 tablet by mouth every day.
Warnings: Do not take while driving or operating machinery.
Side effects: May cause dizziness or nausea.

a prescription

A 🔊 **Vocabulary • Medications** Read and listen. Then listen again and repeat.

a painkiller

cold tablets

a nasal spray / a decongestant

eye drops

an antihistamine

cough medicine

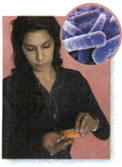
an antibiotic

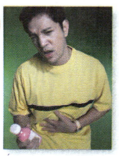
an antacid

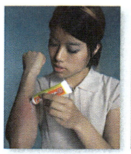
an ointment

vitamins

B Pair work Discuss what you might use each medication for.

> ❝ I might take an antacid for a stomachache. ❞

LISTENING COMPREHENSION

A 🔊 **Listen for key details** Listen to each conversation with a doctor. Use the medications Vocabulary above and the symptoms Vocabulary from page 16 to complete the chart for each patient.

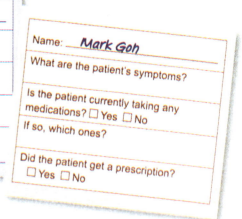

Name: **Didem Yilmaz**
What are the patient's symptoms?
Is the patient currently taking any medications? ☐ Yes ☐ No
If so, which ones?
Did the patient get a prescription? ☐ Yes ☐ No

Name: **Lucy Fernández**
What are the patient's symptoms?
Is the patient currently taking any medications? ☐ Yes ☐ No
If so, which ones?
Did the patient get a prescription? ☐ Yes ☐ No

Name: **Mark Goh**
What are the patient's symptoms?
Is the patient currently taking any medications? ☐ Yes ☐ No
If so, which ones?
Did the patient get a prescription? ☐ Yes ☐ No

B 🔊 **Listen for more details** Listen again. Complete the information about each patient.

Didem Yilmaz
Dosage: One tablet _____ a day
Side effects: ☐ Yes ☐ No
If so, what are they? _____
_____

Lucy Fernández
Dosage: _____ a day
Side effects: ☐ Yes ☐ No
If so, what are they? _____
_____

Mark Goh
Dosage: Apply ointment _____ a day
Side effects: ☐ Yes ☐ No
If so, what are they? _____
_____

NOW YOU CAN Talk about medications

A Preparation Imagine you are visiting the doctor. Complete the patient information form.

B Group work With three other classmates, role-play a visit to a doctor. First, choose roles. Then role-play the three scenes below. Use the patient information form.

Roles
- a patient
- a friend, colleague, classmate, or relative
- a receptionist
- a doctor

Scene 1: The colleague, classmate, friend, or relative recommends a doctor.
Scene 2: The patient calls the receptionist to make an appointment.
Scene 3: The doctor asks about the symptoms and recommends medication, etc.

Patient Information Form

Last name	First name

1. What are your symptoms?
☐ dizziness ☐ coughing ☐ nausea ☐ weakness
☐ sneezing ☐ vomiting ☐ shortness of breath
☐ wheezing ☐ pain (where?)
☐ other:

2. How long have you had these symptoms?

3. Are you currently taking any medications? ☐ Yes ☐ No
If so, which ones?

4. Are you allergic to any medications? ☐ Yes ☐ No
If so, which ones?

♻️ **Be sure to recycle this language.**

Scene 1
I've been [wheezing / coughing / dizzy].
I'm in a lot of pain.
Could you recommend ___?
I think you should try ___.
Why don't you ___?
You may have to ___.
I hope you feel better soon.

Scene 2
I need to make an appointment for ___.
I wonder if I might be able to ___.
Let me check.
Let's see if I can fit you in.
Would you be able to be here ___?
I really appreciate it.

Scene 3
Thanks for fitting me in.
Luckily, I had a cancellation.
Let's have a look.
Are you taking any medications?
Are you allergic to any medications?
Are there any side effects?
Call me tomorrow.

C Presentation Perform your role play for the class.

Review

A 🔊 **Listening comprehension** Listen to each conversation and complete the statements. Then listen again to check your answers.

The patient lost .... when she was eating ....

The patient has .... She needs to take ....

The patient needs .... of his ....

The patient would like to try .... for pain in her ....

B Suggest a medication for each person. (Answers will vary.)

1 ....   2 ....   3 ....   4 ....   5 ....

C Complete each conversation by drawing your own conclusion with <u>must</u>.

1 A: I feel really nauseous. I've been vomiting all morning.
   B: You *must feel terrible* .

2 A: My dentist can't fit me in till next month.
   B: Your dentist ....

3 A: My daughter was sick, but it wasn't anything serious, thank goodness.
   B: You ....

4 A: My husband fell down and broke his ankle.
   B: He .... !

D On a separate sheet of paper, rewrite each statement, using <u>may</u> (or <u>might</u>) and <u>be able to</u>.

1 Maybe the doctor can see you tomorrow.
2 Maybe an acupuncturist can help you.
3 Maybe the hotel can recommend a good dentist.
4 Maybe she can't come to the office before 6:00.
5 Maybe you can buy an antihistamine in the hotel gift shop.

> *The doctor might be able to see you tomorrow.*

🎵 **Top Notch Pop**
"X-ray of My Heart"
Lyrics p. 149

E **Writing** On a separate sheet of paper, compare two types of medical treatments. Use the Reading on page 20 and your own experiences and ideas. Consider the following questions:

- How are the two medical treatments similar or different?
- Which treatment do you think is more effective?
- Why might people choose each treatment?
- Which treatments do you—or people you know—use? Why?

WRITING BOOSTER • p. 141
- Comparisons and contrasts
- Guidance for Exercise E

ORAL REVIEW

Pair work

1 Create a conversation for the people in the photos to the left. Start like this:

I'm afraid I'm not going to be able to come in today. I . . .

2 Create a conversation for the man on the phone and the receptionist in the doctor's office below. Make an appointment. Start like this:

A: Hello. Can I help you?
B: I wonder if I might be able to . . .

Game Each student takes a turn describing the doctor's office below, using <u>must</u> or <u>may</u> and <u>might</u>. (If a student can't say anything, he or she is out.) For example:

He's touching his arm. He must be in a lot of pain.

NOW I CAN... ✓

- ☐ Call in sick.
- ☐ Make a medical or dental appointment.
- ☐ Discuss types of treatments.
- ☐ Talk about medications.

UNIT 3
Preview
Getting Things Done

GOALS After Unit 3, you will be able to:
1. Get someone else to do something.
2. Request express service.
3. Evaluate the quality of service.
4. Plan a meeting or social event.

Are you a PROCRASTINATOR?
Take the survey.

1. At the beginning of every week, you ___.
   - a. always make to-do lists for your calendar
   - b. sometimes make to-do lists, but you often forget
   - c. don't bother with planning and just let things happen

2. When you need to buy someone a gift, you ___.
   - a. get something right away
   - b. buy something a few days before you have to give it
   - c. pick something up on the day you have to give it

3. When you have something that's broken, you ___.
   - a. immediately take it in to be repaired
   - b. wait for a convenient time to take it in
   - c. never get around to taking it in

4. When you have a lot of things you need to do, you do ___.
   - a. the hardest things first
   - b. the easiest things first
   - c. anything but what you need to do

5. When you need to get something done in a short amount of time, you ___.
   - a. feel motivated to work even harder
   - b. feel a little nervous, but you get to work
   - c. have a hard time doing it

6. You ___ feel bad when there are things you haven't gotten done yet.
   - a. always
   - b. sometimes
   - c. rarely

Your results

If you answered "c" four or more times:
You are a classic procrastinator! You tend to put things off.

If you answered "b" four or more times:
You are a bit of a procrastinator, but you try to get things done on time.

If you answered "a" four or more times:
You are organized and self-motivated. You never put off what you can get done now.

Source: adapted from www.blogthings.com.

A Pair work Compare responses on the survey with a partner. Does your score accurately describe the kind of person you are? Explain, using examples.

B Discussion Based on the survey questions, what is a procrastinator? What do you think it means to be an "organized and self-motivated" person? What do you think are the advantages of being that type of person?

C **Photo story** Read and listen to some customers placing orders at a copy shop.

English For Today's World — connecting people from different cultures and language backgrounds

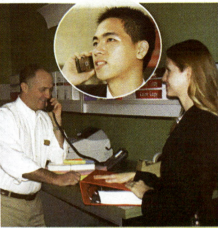

Manager: What can I do for you today, Ms. Krauss?
Customer 1: I need to get these documents copied a.s.a.p.* Think I could get 300 copies done by 11:00?
Manager: I'm afraid that might be difficult. I've got a lot of orders to complete this morning.
Customer 1: Sorry. I know this is last minute. But it's really urgent.
Manager: Well, you're a good customer. Let me see what I can do.
Customer 1: Thanks a million. You're a lifesaver!

Manager: Excuse me . . . Hello. Happy Copy.
Customer 2: Hi, Sam. Ken Li here.
Manager: Hi, Mr. Li. How can I help you today?
Customer 2: Well, I'm going through my to-do list, and I just realized I need to get fifty 30-page sales binders made up for our meeting next week. Any chance I could get them done by first thing tomorrow morning?
Manager: Tomorrow morning? No sweat. Can you get the documents to me before noon?
Customer 2: Absolutely. I owe you one, Sam!

Manager: Sorry to keep you waiting, Ms. Krauss.
Customer 1: Well, I see that you've got a lot on your plate today. I won't keep you any longer.
Manager: Don't worry, Ms. Krauss. We'll get your order done on time.
Customer 1: Should I give you a call later?
Manager: No need for that. Come at 11:00 and I'll have your documents ready.
Customer 1: Thanks, Sam.

*a.s.a.p. = as soon as possible

Customer 2: Chinese speaker

D Paraphrase Say each of the following statements from the Photo Story in your <u>own</u> way.

1 "... this is last minute."
2 "... it's really urgent."
3 "You're a lifesaver!"
4 "No sweat."
5 "I owe you one!"
6 "... you've got a lot on your plate ..."
7 "I won't keep you any longer."

E Discussion Based on the survey on page 26, how would you describe each character in the Photo Story? Complete the chart. Then compare charts with your classmates.

	Procrastinator?	Organized?	Explain
Ms. Krauss	☐	☐	
Sam	☐	☐	
Mr. Li	☐	☐	

LESSON 1

GOAL Get someone else to do something

GRAMMAR *Causatives get, have, and make*

Use a causative to express the idea that one person causes another to do something.

Get: Use an object and an infinitive.

object	infinitive
I got **the company**	**to agree** to a new date for the meeting.
They got **the students**	**to clean up** after the party.

Have: Use an object and the base form of a verb.

object	base form
I had **my assistant**	**plan** the meeting.
They had **the bellman**	**bring** the guests' bags to their rooms.

Make: Use an object and the base form of a verb.

object	base form
I made **my brother**	**help** me finish the job.
They made **him**	**sign** the form.

Causatives: meaning
- The causative <u>get</u> implies that someone convinced another person to do something.
- The causative <u>have</u> implies that instructions were given.
- The causative <u>make</u> implies an obligation.

GRAMMAR BOOSTER ▸ p. 125
- *Let* to indicate permission
- Causative *have*: common errors

Grammar practice Complete each sentence with a causative.

1 (have / call) Why don't you …… your assistant ………… them?
2 (get / do) I'll never be able to …… my brother ………… the laundry.
3 (have / clean) Why didn't you …… your friends ………… up after the party?
4 (get / give) You should …… the hotel ………… you your money back.
5 (make / wash) Why don't you …… your brother ………… the dishes?
6 (get / sign) I'm sure we can …… the teacher ………… these forms.

VOCABULARY *Some ways to help out another person*

A 🔊 2:03 Read and listen. Then listen again and repeat.

My car's at the repair shop. Could you possibly **give me a ride** to work?	I need to use the men's room. Could you **keep an eye on** my things till I get back?	Excuse me. Would you mind **lending** me your pen?	I can't play soccer this afternoon. You're a good player. Do you think you could **fill in for** me?	I'm too busy to go out for lunch. Do you think you could **pick up** a sandwich for me?

give [someone] **a ride** | **keep an eye on** [something or someone] | **lend** [someone] [something] | **fill in for** [someone] | **pick up** [something or someone]

B Complete each sentence with one of the verb phrases from the Vocabulary.

1. The meeting doesn't end until 5:00. Do you think you could .... my kids from school at 4:00?
2. Janus usually answers the phones but he's out sick today. Could you possibly .... him?
3. Oops. I'm completely out of cash! Do you think you could .... me some money for lunch?
4. I have to make an important phone call. Could you .... my daughter for about ten minutes?
5. Doris is catching a flight at 9:00. Do you think you might be able to .... her .... to the airport?

CONVERSATION MODEL

A 🔊 2:04 Read and listen to someone asking for a favor.

A: Martin, I wonder if you could do me a favor.
B: Sure. What do you need?
A: My car's at the repair shop and I need to pick it up at 3:00. Do you think you could give me a ride?
B: I would, but I have a doctor's appointment at 2:00.
A: Oh, that's OK. I understand.
B: Maybe you could get Jack to take you.
A: Good idea.

🔊 2:06 **Ways to indicate acceptance**
I understand.
No problem.
Don't worry about it.

B 🔊 2:05 **Rhythm and intonation** Listen again and repeat. Then practice the Conversation Model with a partner.

NOW YOU CAN   Get someone else to do something

I wonder if you could do me a favor . . .

A Review the Vocabulary. On a separate sheet of paper, write a list of three requests for a favor.

B **Pair work** Change the Conversation Model to create a new conversation. Use one of the favors from your list. Your partner gives a reason for turning down your request and suggests getting someone else to do it. Then change roles.

A: ...., I wonder if you could do me a favor.
B: .... What do you need?
A: .... Do you think you could ....?
B: I would, but ....
A: Oh, that's OK. ....
B: Maybe you could get ....
A: ....

Reasons to turn down a request
• I'm running late for an appointment.
• I have a meeting in an hour.
• I'm expecting an important phone call.
• Your own reason: ___

Don't stop! Make other suggestions.
What about ___ ?
Why don't you ask ___ ?

C **Change partners** Try to get someone else to do you a favor.

LESSON 2

GOAL Request express service

VOCABULARY Services

A 🔊 Read and listen. Then listen again and repeat.

1 dry-clean a suit

2 repair shoes

3 frame a picture

4 deliver a package

5 lengthen / shorten a skirt

6 print a sign

7 copy a report

B Pair work Name other things you can get these services for.

> " You can also dry-clean sweaters or pants. "

GRAMMAR The passive causative

Use a form of <u>have</u> or <u>get</u> with an object and a past participle to talk about arranging services. There is no difference in meaning between <u>have</u> and <u>get</u>.

	object	past participle
I had	my suits	dry-cleaned.
They're having	the office	painted tomorrow.
She can get	her sandals	repaired in an hour.

Remember: In the passive voice, a <u>by</u> phrase is used when the information is important.
We had the office painted last week. It looks great. (no <u>by</u> phrase)
We're having the office painted **by Royal Painting Services**. They're the best!

GRAMMAR BOOSTER ▶ p. 126
• The passive causative: the <u>by</u> phrase

A Grammar practice Write questions using the passive causative. Write three questions with <u>have</u> and three with <u>get</u>.

1 Would it be possible to / these pictures / frame?

2 Could I / these sandals / repair / here?

3 Where can I / this bowl / gift wrap?

4 Can I / these shirts / dry-clean / by tomorrow?

5 Is it possible to / my hair / cut / at 3:00 / by George?

6 Would you / these photos / print / before 6:00?

30 UNIT 3

B 🔊 **Listening comprehension** Listen to the conversations. Complete each statement with the item and the service. Use passive causatives.

1 She needs to get her ....
2 He wants to get his ....
3 She's thinking about having a ....
4 He needs to have his ....

CONVERSATION MODEL

A 🔊 Read and listen to someone requesting express service.

A: Do you think I could get this jacket dry-cleaned by tomorrow?
B: Tomorrow? That might be difficult.
A: I'm sorry, but it's pretty urgent. My friend is getting married this weekend.
B: Well, I'll see what I can do. But it won't be ready until after 4:00.
A: I really appreciate it. Thanks!

B 🔊 **Rhythm and intonation** Listen again and repeat. Then practice the Conversation Model with a partner.

NOW YOU CAN Request express service

A Pair work Change the Conversation Model. Use the ideas to request an express service and give a reason for why it's urgent. Then change roles.

A: Do you think I could .... by .... ?
B: .... ? That might be difficult.
A: I'm sorry, but it's pretty urgent. ....
B: Well, I'll see what I can do. But it won't be ready until ....
A: .... !

Ideas for express services
- frame a [photo / painting / drawing / diploma]
- dry-clean a [suit / dress / sweater]
- lengthen or shorten a [dress / skirt / pants]

Ideas for why it's urgent
- Someone is coming to visit.
- You're going on [a vacation / a business trip].
- There's going to be [a party / a meeting].
- Your own idea: ___

Don't stop!
- Say you need to have the service completed earlier.
- Ask how much it will cost.

 Be sure to recycle this language.

I owe you one!   I know this is last minute.
Thanks a million.   I won't keep you any longer.
You're a lifesaver!

B Change partners Request other express services.

LESSON 3

GOAL: Evaluate the quality of service

BEFORE YOU READ

Warm-up Have you or someone you know ever had something custom-made—for example, something to wear or something for your home? If so, how was the quality of workmanship?

READING 2:11

The Tailors of Hong Kong

The famous Hong Kong 24-hour suit is a thing of the past, but tailors there are still reliable: You can trust them if they say they'll have your clothes custom-made in just a few days.

Today, prices are quite reasonable—not as low as they used to be, but they're often about what you'd pay for a ready-made garment back home. The difference, of course, is that a tailor-made garment should fit you perfectly. Most tailors are extremely professional. The workmanship and quality of the better established shops rival even those of London's Savile Row—but at less than half the price!

Tailors in Hong Kong are very helpful and are willing to make almost any garment you want. Most offer a wide range of fabrics from which to choose, from cotton and linen to very fine wools, cashmere, and silk.

At your first fitting, the tailor will take your measurements.

You should allow three to five days to have a garment custom-made, with at least two or three fittings. You will pay a deposit of about 50% up front. But if you are not satisfied with the finished product, you don't have to accept it. Your only expense will be the deposit.

With more than 2,500 tailoring establishments in Hong Kong, it shouldn't be any problem finding one. Some of the most famous are located in hotel arcades and shopping complexes, but the more upscale the location, the higher the prices.

Once you've had something custom-made and your tailor has your measurements, you will more than likely be able to order additional clothing online, even after you've returned home!

You can choose from a variety of fabrics.

Tailors will make almost any garment you want—suits, evening gowns, wedding dresses, leather jackets, and shirts.

Source: Information from *Frommer's Hong Kong*

A Identify supporting details Check the statements that are true, according to the article. Find information in the Reading to support your answers.

1. ☐ You used to be able to get a suit made in one day in Hong Kong.
2. ☐ Having a suit custom-made in Hong Kong is always less expensive than buying one at home.
3. ☐ If you buy a garment on Savile Row in London, you will pay about twice as much as you would pay for one custom-made in Hong Kong.
4. ☐ If you are not satisfied with the finished garment, you can refuse to accept it and pay only 50% of the total cost.
5. ☐ If you want to pay a lower price for a custom-made garment, go to an upscale hotel shopping arcade.

32 UNIT 3

B **Activate language from a text** Find these adjectives in the Reading on page 32. Complete the descriptions, using the adjectives.

> reliable   reasonable   helpful   professional

1. I find Portello's to be really .... compared to other places. I've shopped around and I can't find another service with such low prices.
2. What I like about Link Copy Services is that they're so .... Even if the job is a bit unusual, they're willing to try.
3. Jamco Design is extremely .... You never have to worry about their doing anything less than an excellent job.
4. Dom's Auto Repair is incredibly .... If they promise to have a job ready in an hour, you can be sure that they will.

On your *ActiveBook* Self-Study Disc: **Extra Reading Comprehension Questions**

PRONUNCIATION Emphatic stress to express enthusiasm

2:12

Read and listen. Then listen again and repeat. Finally, read each statement on your own, using emphatic stress.

1. They're REALly reliable.
2. They're inCREDibly helpful.
3. They're exTREMEly professional.
4. They're SO reasonable.

NOW YOU CAN Evaluate the quality of service

Reasons for choosing a business
- speed
- reliability
- price
- workmanship
- location
- efficiency
- professionalism
- other: ___

A **Frame your ideas** Complete the chart with services you or someone you know uses. Write the name of the business and list the reasons why you use that business. Then compare charts with a partner.

Service	Name of business	Reason
laundry / dry cleaning		
repairs		
tailoring		
delivery		
haircuts		
copying		
other: _____		

B **Discussion** Recommend local businesses from your chart. Explain why you or other people use them. Use the active and passive causatives.

> "I always get my clothes dry-cleaned at Quick Clean. They're near my home and their prices are reasonable."

> "I rarely have my shoes repaired. But I hear that Al's Shoes is fast and reliable."

LESSON 4

GOAL Plan a meeting or social event

BEFORE YOU LISTEN

A 🔊 **Vocabulary** • *Planning an event* Read and listen. Then listen again and repeat.

make a list of attendees

pick a date, time, and place

make a budget

assign responsibilities

plan an agenda

send out an announcement

arrange catering

set up the room

B **Pair work** Have you ever taken any of these steps to plan an event, such as a meeting or party? Which of the activities do you think you would be the best at doing? Use the Vocabulary.

LISTENING COMPREHENSION

A 🔊 **Listen for main ideas** Listen to the conversation and answer the questions.

1. What kind of event are they planning?
   ....
2. How many people will come to the event?
   ....
3. Is it a formal or informal event?
   ....
4. Which of the following are mentioned as part of the event? (music / food / a lecture / dancing / meetings)
   ....

B 🔊 **Listen for order of details** Listen again and number the activities in the order they will occur. Circle the activities she'll do herself.

	make a list of attendees
1	pick a date and time
	pick a location
	make a budget
	assign responsibilities
	send out announcements
	arrange catering
	arrange music
	set up the room

34   UNIT 3

NOW YOU CAN Plan a meeting or a social event

A Frame your ideas Take the survey. Compare answers with a partner.

Check which event activities you would rather do. Choose from Column A or B.

What type of person are YOU?

Column A	Column B
○ make a budget	○ spend money
○ assign responsibilities	○ take responsibility
○ plan an agenda	○ be a presenter
○ arrange catering	○ cook food
○ get people to set up the room	○ set up the room
○ leave before cleanup	○ stick around to clean up

If you chose four or more from Column A, you're a **BORN ORGANIZER!**

If you chose four or more from Column B, you're a **TEAM PLAYER!**

B Notepadding In a group, plan a meeting or social event for your class. Choose the type of event and discuss what needs to be done. Write the activities and assign responsibilities. Discuss dates, times, and locations.

Type of event:
Date and time:
Location:

Activity	Name

Some ideas

- A special meeting
- An English practice day

An end-of-year ⎫
New Year's Eve ⎬ party
A TGIF*   ⎭
*Thank goodness it's Friday!

A talent   ⎫
A *Top Notch Pop* karaoke ⎬ show

♻ **Be sure to recycle this language.**

Why don't we ___ ? | What needs to be done [first]?
Why don't you ___ ? | That's a [good idea. / great idea. /
How about ___ ? | good point.]
What about ___ ? | That would be great.
I think ___ . | That sounds ___ .

C Discussion Present your plans to your class. Then choose the best plan.

Review

grammar · vocabulary · listening
reading · speaking · pronunciation

A 🔊 **Listening comprehension** Listen to each conversation. Write a sentence to describe what the customer needs and when. Listen again if necessary.

Example: He'd like to get his shoes shined by tomorrow morning.

1 ....
2 ....
3 ....
4 ....

B Complete each question or request with any noun that makes sense with the passive causative verb.

1 Can I get my .... dry-cleaned by tomorrow?
2 I'd like to have this .... lengthened.
3 Where can I get this .... shortened?
4 Can you tell me where I can get some .... copied?
5 Where did she get her .... framed?
6 How much did he pay to have his .... repaired?
7 What's the best place to get some .... printed?
8 Where can I go to get my .... delivered quickly?

🎵 **Top Notch Pop**
"I'll Get Back to You"
Lyrics p. 149

C Complete each causative statement in your own way. Remember to use either the base form or the infinitive form of a verb.

1 At the end of the meal, she had the waiter ....
2 We got the travel agent ....
3 When I was young, my mother always made me ....
4 When you arrive, you should get the hotel ....
5 Don't forget to have the gas station attendant ....
6 I can never get my friends ....

D **Writing** Do you think being a procrastinator is a serious problem? On a separate sheet of paper, explain your views by giving examples from personal experience.

Some possible examples
- getting things repaired
- having things cleaned
- paying bills
- making plans for a vacation
- keeping in touch with people

WRITING BOOSTER ▸ p. 142
- Supporting an opinion with personal examples
- Guidance for Exercise D

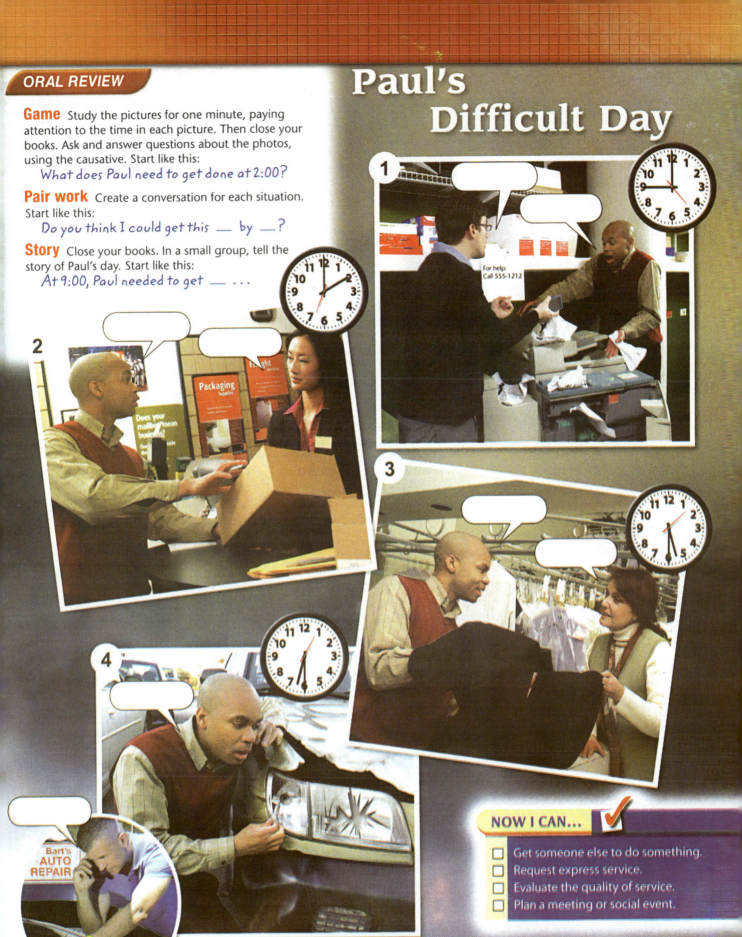

UNIT 4

Reading for Pleasure

Preview

GOALS After Unit 4, you will be able to:
1 Recommend a book.
2 Offer to lend something.
3 Describe your reading habits.
4 Discuss the quality of reading materials.

Looking for a good classic? Check out our recommendations. Click on a category for more.

search | help | feedback

FICTION

Novels

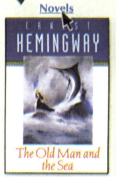

Hemingway's exquisite novel. Read and reread by millions!

Mysteries

Who killed Charles McCarthy at the pool? And why? Detective Sherlock Holmes tries to solve another case.

Thrillers

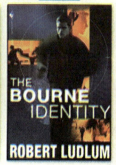

A contemporary thriller that will have you on the edge of your seat!

Romance

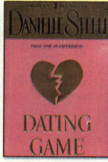

No one does romance like Danielle Steele.

Science fiction

A strange object is found on the Moon. But who put it there? Arthur Clarke's masterpiece!

Short stories

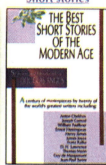

Beautiful short stories by the world's greatest and most beloved writers.

NON-FICTION

Biographies

The true story of the amazing woman who inspired millions.

Autobiographies

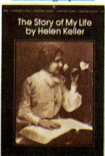

In Helen Keller's own words—her unforgettable story.

Travel

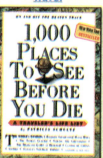

A must-read for real travelers—or even those who just dream about traveling!

Memoirs

The true story of writer Frank McCourt's surprising and funny experiences as a teacher in New York City.

Self-help

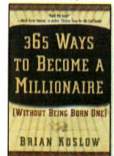

Want to get rich? Brian Koslow shows you how.

A 🔊 **Vocabulary • Types of books** Read and listen. Then listen again and repeat.

fiction		non-fiction	
a novel	a romance novel	a biography	a memoir
a mystery	science fiction	an autobiography	a self-help book
a thriller	short stories	a travel book	

B Discussion Do you prefer fiction or non-fiction? Have you ever read a book in English? How about a magazine or a newspaper? If not, what would you like to read? Why?

C 🔊 2:20 **Photo story** Read and listen to a conversation between two friends at a bookstore.

Lynn: Hey, Sophie! I've never run into you here before!
Sophie: Lynn! Good to see you. Looking for anything special?
Lynn: No, I'm just browsing. How about you?
Sophie: I'm just picking up some gardening magazines for my mom. She can't get enough of them . . . So, anything interesting?

Lynn: This one doesn't look bad. It's a biography of Helen Keller. What about you? Are you reading anything good these days?
Sophie: Well, I've got a new mystery on my night table, but I can't seem to get into it. I guess mysteries just aren't my thing.
Lynn: I know what you mean. They put me to sleep.
Sophie: Well, you're a big reader. I wonder if you could recommend something for me.

Lynn: Have you read the new John Grisham thriller?
Sophie: No, I haven't. I didn't know he had a new book out.
Lynn: Well, I can't put it down. It's a real page-turner.
Sophie: Thanks for the tip! Do you think I could borrow it when you're done with it?
Lynn: Of course. If you can wait till the end of the week, I'd be happy to lend it to you.

D **Think and explain** Classify each of the six underlined expressions from the Photo Story by its meaning. Explain your choices.

Likes	Doesn't like

E **Paraphrase** Say each of the underlined verbs and phrasal verbs in your own way.
1 I've never <u>run into</u> you here before.
2 I'm just <u>browsing</u>.
3 I'm <u>picking up</u> some gardening magazines for my mom.
4 Do you think I could <u>borrow</u> it when you're finished?
5 I'd be happy to <u>lend</u> it to you.

F **Group work** What percentage of your total reading time do you spend on the following reading materials? (Make sure it adds up to 100%!) Compare percentages with your classmates.

magazines		fiction	
newspapers		non-fiction	
the Internet		other	

LESSON 1

GOAL Recommend a book

VOCABULARY Ways to describe a book

A Read and listen. Then listen again and repeat.

It's **a page-turner.** *It's so interesting that you want to keep reading it.*
It's **a cliff-hanger.** *It's so exciting that you can't wait to find out what happens next.*
It's **a best-seller.** *It's very popular and everyone is buying copies.*
It's **a fast read.** *It's easy and enjoyable to read.*
It's **hard to follow.** *It's difficult to understand.*
It's **trash.** *It's very poor quality.*

B Pair work Discuss which types of books you find the most interesting. Use the Vocabulary from here and page 38.

> " I prefer thrillers. A thriller is usually a pretty fast read. It helps pass the time. "

GRAMMAR Noun clauses

A noun clause is a group of words that functions as a noun. A noun clause can be introduced by <u>that</u> and often functions as the direct object of a "mental activity" verb.

I didn't know **that he wrote that book.**
I think **that Junot Diaz's novels are fantastic.**
She forgot **that Andrew Morton wrote biographies.**

When a noun clause functions as a direct object, <u>that</u> may be omitted.

I didn't know **he wrote that book.**

In short answers, use <u>so</u> to replace a noun clause after the verbs <u>think</u>, <u>believe</u>, <u>guess</u>, and <u>hope</u>.

A: Does Steven King have a new book out?
B: I think **so**. / I believe **so**. / I guess **so**. / I hope **so**.
(so = that Steven King has a new book out)

Other clauses with <u>that</u> often follow certain predicate adjectives. The word <u>that</u> can be omitted.

We're both **disappointed** (that) his new book isn't very good.
Were you **surprised** (that) the ending was sad?

Noun clauses and other clauses with <u>that</u> often follow these verbs and adjectives.

Verbs		Adjectives
agree	hear	disappointed
think	see	happy
believe	understand	sad
feel	hope	sorry
suppose	forget	sure
doubt	remember	surprised
guess	know	

Be careful!
I don't think **so**. / I don't believe **so**.
BUT I guess **not**. / I hope **not**.
NOT ~~I don't guess so.~~ / ~~I don't hope so.~~

GRAMMAR BOOSTER ▸ p. 126
• More verbs and adjectives that can be followed by clauses with <u>that</u>

Grammar practice On a separate sheet of paper, respond to each question with a clause using <u>that</u>. Use the prompts.

What has the author Monica Ali been up to lately? (write / a new novel)

I think that she has written a new novel.

1 Where does the story take place? (in London / I guess)
2 What does Amy Tan usually write about? (mother-daughter relationships / I believe)
3 Where does Mario Vargas Llosa's novel *The Feast of the Goat* take place? (in the Dominican Republic / I hear)
4 What kind of book is Dan Brown going to write next? (another thriller / I hope)

PRONUNCIATION Sentence stress in short answers with *so*

A 🔊 Read and listen. Notice the stress on the verb in short answers with <u>so</u>. Then listen again and repeat.

1. Are there a lot of characters in the story? — I THINK so.
2. Has she read that book yet? — I don't THINK so.
3. Do you think this thriller will be good? — I HOPE so.
4. Does the story have a happy ending? — I beLIEVE so.

B **Pair work** Ask and answer <u>yes</u> / <u>no</u> questions about your future plans. Respond with short answers, using <u>think</u>, <u>believe</u>, <u>hope</u>, or <u>guess</u>.

"Are you going to read anything this weekend?" "I think so."

CONVERSATION MODEL

A 🔊 Read and listen to someone recommend a book.

A: Have you been reading anything interesting lately?
B: Actually, I'm reading a thriller called *Don't Close Your Eyes*.
A: I've never heard of that one. Is it any good?
B: Oh, I think it's great. It's a cliff-hanger. How about you?
A: I've just finished a Hemingway novel, *The Old Man and the Sea*. I highly recommend it.

B 🔊 **Rhythm and intonation** Listen again and repeat. Then practice the Conversation Model with a partner.

NOW YOU CAN Recommend a book

A **Notepadding** Write some notes about a book you've read, or choose one of the books here.

- Type of book:
- Title:
- Author:
- What is it about?
- Your recommendation:

FICTION

The Interpreter by Charles Randolph
Silvia Broome is an interpreter at the United Nations who hears a secret plan to kill a state leader. But is she telling the truth?

The Time Machine by H. G. Wells
A man builds a time machine and goes into the future, where he finds that people have become fearful, child-like creatures. But what are they afraid of?

NON-FICTION

New York by Vicki Stripton
Every year, millions of tourists visit "the city that never sleeps." Read about its history, its sights, and its people.

Martin Luther King by Coleen Degnan-Veness
In the U.S. in the 1950s and 60s, blacks did not have equal rights. But Martin Luther King had a dream —blacks and whites living together happily. He led peaceful protests and changed the country—and the world.

B **Pair work** Change the Conversation Model, using the Vocabulary and your notepad.

A: Have you been reading anything interesting lately?
B: Actually, ...
A: .... heard of that one. Is it any good?
B: Oh, I think .... It's .... How about you?
A: ....

Don't stop!
Ask questions about the book.
What's it about?
Where does it take place?
Why did you decide to read it?

LESSON 2

GOAL Offer to lend something

CONVERSATION MODEL

A 🔊 2:25 Read and listen to someone offering to lend a magazine.

A: Is that the latest issue of *Car Magazine*?
B: Yes, it is.
A: Could you tell me where you bought it? I can't find it anywhere.
B: At the newsstand across the street. But I think it's sold out.
A: Too bad. There's an article in there I'm dying to read.
B: You know, I'd be happy to lend it to you when I'm done with it.
A: Really? That would be great. Thanks!

B 🔊 2:26 **Rhythm and intonation** Listen again and repeat. Then practice the Conversation Model with a partner.

GRAMMAR Noun clauses: embedded questions

GRAMMAR BOOSTER ▶ p. 127
- Embedded questions:
  ○ usage and common errors
  ○ punctuation
  ○ with infinitives
- Noun clauses as subjects and objects

Noun clauses sometimes include embedded questions. Use **if** or **whether** to begin embedded **yes / no** questions. (**If** and **whether** have the same meaning.)

Yes / no questions	Embedded yes / no questions
Is that magazine any good?	Tell me **if that magazine is any good**.
Did he like the article?	I'd like to know **whether he liked the article**.
Have you finished that newspaper?	Could you tell me **if you've finished that newspaper**?
Can I borrow your brochure?	I wonder **whether I could borrow your brochure**.

Use a question word to begin embedded information questions.

Information questions	Embedded information questions
What's the article about?	Tell me **what the article's about**.
Why did you decide to read it?	Could you tell me **why you decided to read it**?
Who's the writer?	I wonder **who the writer is**.
Who recommended the article?	Do you know **who recommended the article**?
Who(m) is it written for?	Can you tell me **who(m) it's written for**?
Whose magazine is it?	I'd like to know **whose magazine it is**.
When was it written?	Would you tell me **when it was written**?
Where is the writer from?	Do you know **where the writer is from**?

Be careful!
Use normal word order (not question word order) in embedded questions.
Don't say:
  I wonder ~~who is~~ the writer.
  Do you know ~~where is~~ the writer from?

A Find the grammar Underline three examples of noun clauses in the Photo Story on page 39. Which two are embedded questions?

B Grammar practice Change the questions to embedded questions.

1 Does she like to read?
  I wonder ....

2 Where did you get that magazine?
  Can you tell me .... ?

3 Is he a John Grisham fan?
  I've been wondering ....

4 Why don't you read newspapers?
  I'm curious ....

5 Who told you about the article?
  I was wondering ....

6 When did you hear about the new website?
  I'd like to know ....

C Pair work Complete the survey below. Then look at your partner's responses. Use embedded questions to learn more about your partner.

" Tell me why you like to read photography magazines. "

" I wonder what sections of the newspaper you like to read. "

What kinds of materials do you like to read?

MAGAZINES

- ○ World news
- ○ Sports
- ○ Photography
- ○ Computers and electronics
- ○ Entertainment
- ○ Music
- ○ Fashion
- ○ Economics
- ○ Health and fitness
- ○ Business
- ○ Food and cooking
- ○ Other _____

NEWSPAPER SECTIONS

- ○ World news
- ○ Local news
- ○ Sports
- ○ Business
- ○ Entertainment
- ○ Travel
- ○ Other _____

NOW YOU CAN | Offer to lend something

A Pair work Change the Conversation Model. Create a conversation in which you offer to lend your partner something that you are reading. Then change roles.

A: Is that .... ?

B: Yes, ...

A: Could you tell me where you bought it? I can't find it anywhere.

B: .... But I think it's sold out.

A: Too bad. ....

B: You know, I'd be happy to lend it to you when I'm done with it.

A: .... !

Don't stop!
Use more embedded questions.
Could you tell me ___?
Do you know ___?
I wonder ___.

B Change partners Discuss and offer to lend another magazine, newspaper, or book.

LESSON 3

GOAL Describe your reading habits

BEFORE YOU LISTEN

A 🔊 2:27 **Vocabulary** • *Some ways to enjoy reading* Read and listen. Then listen again and repeat.

curl up with [a book]

read aloud [to someone]

listen to audio books

do puzzles

read [articles] online

skim through [a newspaper]

read electronic books / e-books

B Pair work Discuss which activities from the Vocabulary match the situations below. Explain your reasons.

- Is convenient for when you are driving
- Helps pass the time during a bus or train commute
- Is a good way to relax
- Is a way to keep up with the news

LISTENING COMPREHENSION

🔊 2:28 **Listen to take notes** Listen and take notes to answer these questions about each speaker. Listen again if necessary.

1. What kinds of reading material does he or she like?
2. When does he or she like to read?
3. Where does he or she like to read?

Su Yomei • Taiwan

Ignacio Saralegui • Argentina

Vicki Patterson • U.S.A.

NOW YOU CAN Describe your reading habits

A Frame your ideas Complete the questionnaire.

What are your reading habits?

1. Do you consider yourself to be a big reader? Why or why not?

2. Do you have any favorite authors? Who are they?

3. Do you prefer any particular types of books? Which types?

4. Are you a big newspaper reader? What sections of the paper do you prefer to read?

5. Do you read a lot of magazines? What kind?

6. Do you spend a lot of time reading online? Why or why not?

7. Have you ever read aloud to someone? Has anyone ever read aloud to you? When?

8. Do you listen to audio books? If so, do you like them?

9. When and where do you prefer to read the most?

10. Is there anything else you can add about your reading habits?

B Pair work Use the survey to interview your partner about his or her reading habits. Take notes on a separate sheet of paper.

C Group work Now tell your classmates about your partner's reading habits.

> *Ellen prefers to read in bed before she goes to sleep . . .*

 Be sure to recycle this language.

I'd like to know . . .   I guess (that) . . .
Could you tell me . . . ? I think (that) . . .
                           I suppose (that) . . .

LESSON 4

GOAL Discuss the quality of reading materials

BEFORE YOU READ

Warm-up Do you—or does anyone you know—read comics? Do you think there's any value in reading them?

READING

Comics: trash or treasure?

In Japan, they're known as *manga*; in Latin America, *historietas* or *historias em quadrinhos*; in Italy, *fumetti*. Some people call them "graphic novels." But no matter what you call them, comics are a favorite source of reading pleasure for millions in many parts of the world.

In case you're wondering how popular they are, the best-selling comic in the U.S. sells about 4.5 million copies a year. Mexico's comic titles sell over 7 million copies a week. But Japan is by far the leading publisher of comics in the world. *Manga* account for nearly 40 percent of all the books and magazines published in Japan each year.

Ever since comics first appeared, there have been people who have criticized them. In the 1940s and 50s, many people believed that comics were immoral and that they caused bad behavior among young people. Even today, many question whether young people should read them at all.

They argue that reading comics encourages bad reading habits. In more recent years some comics have been criticized for including violence and sexual content.

On the other hand, some educators see comics as a way to get teenagers to choose reading instead of television and video games. And because of the art, a number of educators have argued that comics are a great way to get children to think creatively. Some recent research has suggested that the combination of visuals and text in comics may be one reason young people handle computers and related software so easily.

In many places, comics have been a convenient way to communicate social or political information. For example, in the 1990s, comics were used by the Brazilian health ministry to communicate information about AIDS. In Japan, the Education Ministry calls comics "a part of Japan's national culture, recognized and highly regarded abroad." Comics are increasingly being used for educational purposes, and many publishers there see them as a useful way of teaching history and other subjects.

No matter how you view them, comics remain a guilty pleasure for millions worldwide.

Sources: Associated Press, Ananova News Service, PRNewswire

> Spider-Man® is one of the world's most recognizable and celebrated comic superheroes. Fifteen million Spider-Man comics are sold each year in 75 countries and in 22 languages.

> In Japan, train station newsstands do a booming business selling *manga* during rush hour. And for true addicts, automatic vending machines that sell *manga* are everywhere.

A Recognize points of view List some reasons people criticize comics and defend them, according to the article.

Some reasons people criticize comics	Some reasons people defend comics

46 UNIT 4

B Critical thinking Discuss the following questions.

1. What point of view do you think the writer of the article has about comics? Explain your reasons.
2. Why do you think comics are so popular around the world? Why do you think Japanese *manga* are so popular outside of Japan?
3. Why do you think some people find reading comics "a guilty pleasure"?

On your *ActiveBook* Self-Study Disc:
Extra Reading Comprehension Questions

NOW YOU CAN Discuss the quality of reading materials

A Frame your ideas Complete the chart to explain your opinions about certain reading materials.

Types of materials	Who reads them?	Are they trash?		Your reasons
comics	boys, 12 to 17 years old	Y	N	I think they're violent and sexist.

Types of materials	Who reads them?	Are they trash?		Your reasons
comics		Y	N	
teen magazines		Y	N	
fashion magazines		Y	N	
sports magazines		Y	N	
movie magazines		Y	N	
romance novels		Y	N	
thrillers		Y	N	
horror magazines		Y	N	
sci-fi magazines		Y	N	
online blogs		Y	N	
newspapers		Y	N	
other:		Y	N	

B Pair work Compare the comments you wrote on your charts. Discuss your ideas. Then choose one type of reading material you both agree is trash and one you both agree is not. Prepare to explain your reasons to the class.

C Group work With a partner, compare the quality of two types of reading materials. Explain your reasons to your classmates.

Text-mining (optional):
Underline language in the Reading on page 46 to use in the Group Work.
For example: "Many people question whether..."

♻ **Be sure to recycle this language.**

Express an opinion
I think (that) . . .
I believe (that) . . .
I guess (that) . . .
In my opinion, . . .

Describe materials
I can't put ___ down.
I'm really into ___.
I can't get enough of ___.
They're a fast read.
I can't get into ___.
___ aren't my thing.
___ don't turn me on.
___ are hard to follow.

Review

More Practice
ActiveBook Self-Study Disc

grammar · vocabulary · listening
reading · speaking · pronunciation

A 🔊 **Listening comprehension** Listen to each conversation and write the type of book each person is discussing. Then decide if the person likes the book. Explain your answer.

	Type of book	Likes it?	Explain your answer
1		Y N	
2		Y N	
3		Y N	
4		Y N	

B Write the name of each type of book.

1 A novel about people falling in love: ....
2 A book about a famous person: ....
3 A book that a famous person writes about his or her own life: ....
4 A very exciting novel with people in dangerous situations: ....
5 Books that are about factual information: ....
6 A strange fictional story about the future: ....

🎵 **Top Notch Pop**
"A True Life Story"
Lyrics p. 149

C Use the expressions in the box to change each question to an embedded question. (Use each expression once.)

> I was wondering . . .   Could you tell me . . .   I don't know . . .
> I can't remember . . .   Would you please tell me . . .

1 Where does the story take place?
   ....
2 Who is the main character in the novel?
   ....
3 How much was that newspaper?
   ....
4 How do you say this in English?
   ....
5 What does this word mean?
   ....

D **Writing** On a separate sheet of paper, write a review of something you've read—a book or an article from a magazine, a newspaper, or the Internet.

• Summarize what it was about.
• Make a recommendation to the reader.

WRITING BOOSTER ▸ p. 143
• Summarizing
• Guidance for Exercise D

ORAL REVIEW

Pair work

1 Create a conversation for the man and woman in which he asks about the book she is reading. She makes a recommendation. He asks if he can borrow the book. Start like this:

Are you reading anything interesting?

2 Use the pictures to create a conversation in which the man and woman discuss their reading habits. For example:

I usually like to curl up in bed with a good book.

Game Close your books. Make an "I" statement about the reading habits of the man or woman.
Your partner guesses if it's the man or the woman.
For example:

A: *I like to do the puzzles in the newspaper.*
B: *I think it's the __.*

NOW I CAN...
- Recommend a book.
- Offer to lend something.
- Describe my reading habits.
- Discuss the quality of reading materials.

UNIT 5 Natural Disasters

Preview

GOALS After Unit 5, you will be able to:
1. Convey a message.
2. Report news.
3. Describe natural disasters.
4. Prepare for an emergency.

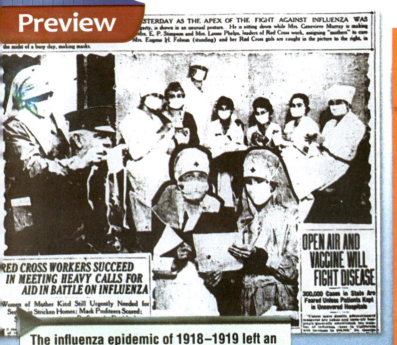

The influenza epidemic of 1918–1919 left an estimated 25 million people dead worldwide.

In February 2010, two major blizzards dumped historic levels of snow on the Washington D.C. area, causing travel delays, school closures, and power outages.

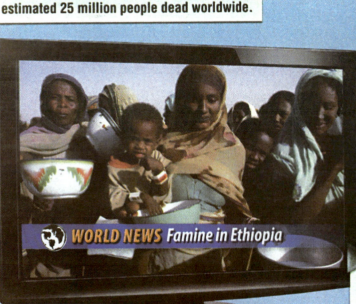

In 1984, hungry communities in Ethiopia faced one of the worst food crises in history.

A Discussion Discuss one or more of the following topics about the content of the news.

1. Do you think or worry about epidemics, famines, and weather emergencies? When stories about these events appear in the news, are you interested in reading about them?
2. Why do newspapers often put this information on the front page?
3. What percentage of the news is about disasters and emergencies?
4. Not all disasters are natural disasters (caused by nature). What are some other kinds of disasters? How are they caused?

B 🔊 **Photo story** Read and listen to a conversation about a natural disaster.

Rachel: Oh, my goodness. Take a look at this!
Tom: Why? What's going on?
Rachel: There's this enormous flood in Slovakia—look at these people on the roof! The water's up to the second floor. And look at these cars. I sure hope there was no one in them.
Tom: That sounds horrendous. Any word on casualties?

Rachel: It says, "No reports of deaths or injuries so far . . . ." But it's in the middle of a city, for goodness sake. The death toll could end up being huge.
Tom: And can you imagine the property damage?
Rachel: Well, they estimate almost 50% of the houses in town are under water already.

Tom: What a disaster!
Rachel: I wonder how this flood compares to the one they had in New Orleans a few years back. Remember that?
Tom: You bet I do. How could anyone forget? And that flooded almost half the city too.
Rachel: Let's turn on CNN. They usually have breaking news about stuff like this.

C **Focus on language** Complete each statement with words or phrases from the Photo Story.

1 Two words that mean very big are .... and ....
2 The number of .... indicates the number of people who are injured or killed in an event.
3 A two-word phrase that means the destruction of or harm to buildings, cars, and other things that belong to victims of an event is ....
4 A two-word expression that is used to describe the first news reports of an important event that is happening at the present is ....

D **Pair work** Where do you get your news? Complete the chart with the news sources you and your partner use.

	My news sources	My partner's news sources
a newspaper		
a weekly news magazine		
TV newscasts		
radio news reports		
Internet news sites		
word of mouth		

E **Discussion** Which do you think are the best sources for breaking news? For weather forecasts? For emergency information? Explain your reasons. Give examples.

LESSON 1

GOAL Convey a message

GRAMMAR Indirect speech: imperatives

To report what someone said without quoting the exact words, use indirect speech. Don't use quotation marks when you write indirect speech.
  Direct speech: Peter said, "Be careful if you go out during the storm."
  Indirect speech: Peter said **to be careful** if you go out during the storm.

An imperative in direct speech becomes an infinitive in indirect speech.
  They said, "**Read** the weather report." → They said **to read** the weather report.
  She says, "**Don't go** out without a full tank of gas." → She says **not to go** out without a full tank of gas.

Change time expressions and pronouns in indirect speech as necessary.
  She told Dan, "Call **me tomorrow**." → She told Dan to call **her the next day**.

Indirect speech is a kind of noun clause. It is the direct object following a reporting verb such as say, tell, or ask.

GRAMMAR BOOSTER ▸ p. 129
• Direct speech: punctuation rules

A Grammar practice On a separate sheet of paper, rewrite each statement in indirect speech, making necessary changes.

1 Martha told me, "Be home before the snowstorm."   *Martha told me to be home before the snowstorm.*
2 Everyone is saying, "Get ready for a big storm."
3 The radio says, "Get supplies of food and water in case the roads are closed."
4 They told her, "Don't be home too late this afternoon."
5 Maria always tells him, "Don't leave your doors open."

B Pair work For each sentence, say what you think the speaker's original words were. Take turns.

1 He told them to call him when it starts raining.   "Please call me when it starts raining."
2 The police said to leave a window or door open when there's going to be a severe storm.
3 She told his parents to read the emergency instructions in the newspaper.
4 Ray told Allison to look for the story about him in the paper the next day.
5 She asked him to pick up some supplies for her on the way home.
6 They told me not to wait until the snow gets heavy.

CONVERSATION MODEL

A 🔊 3:03 Read and listen to someone conveying a message.

A: I'm on the phone with your parents. Would you like to say hello?
B: I would, but I'm running late.
A: Anything you'd like me to tell them?
B: Yes. Please tell them to turn on the TV. There's a storm on the way.
A: Will do.

B 🔊 3:04 **Rhythm and intonation** Listen again and repeat. Then practice the Conversation Model with a partner.

PRONUNCIATION   Direct and indirect speech: rhythm

A 🔊 3:05 Notice the rhythm of sentences in direct and indirect speech. Read and listen. Then listen again and repeat.

1. He said, [pause] "Be home before midnight." → He said to be home before midnight.
2. I told your parents, [pause] "Get a flu shot at the clinic." → I told your parents to get a flu shot at the clinic.

B Pair work Take turns reading aloud the sentences in the Grammar Practice on page 52. Read both the original sentences and the sentences you wrote, using correct rhythm for direct and indirect speech.

NOW YOU CAN   Convey a message

A Notepadding Read the possible excuses and messages. Then write three more excuses and three more messages.

B Pair work Change the Conversation Model. Role-play conveying a message. Use any of the excuses / messages on the telephone display. Then change roles.

A: I'm on the phone with .... Would you like to say hello?
B: I would, but ....
A: Anything you'd like me to tell ....?
B: Yes. Please tell .... to ....
A: ....

Don't stop!
Continue the conversation.
Ask your partner:
• what time he or she will be home.
• to do you a favor.
• to call you later.

C Change partners Practice the conversation again. Use another message. Use another excuse.

Possible excuses
I'm running late.
I have an appointment.
I don't have time.
Your own three excuses:

Possible messages
Watch the news. There's a story about ___ .
Turn on the TV / radio / computer. There's a bad storm on its way.
Call me at the office.
Your own three messages:

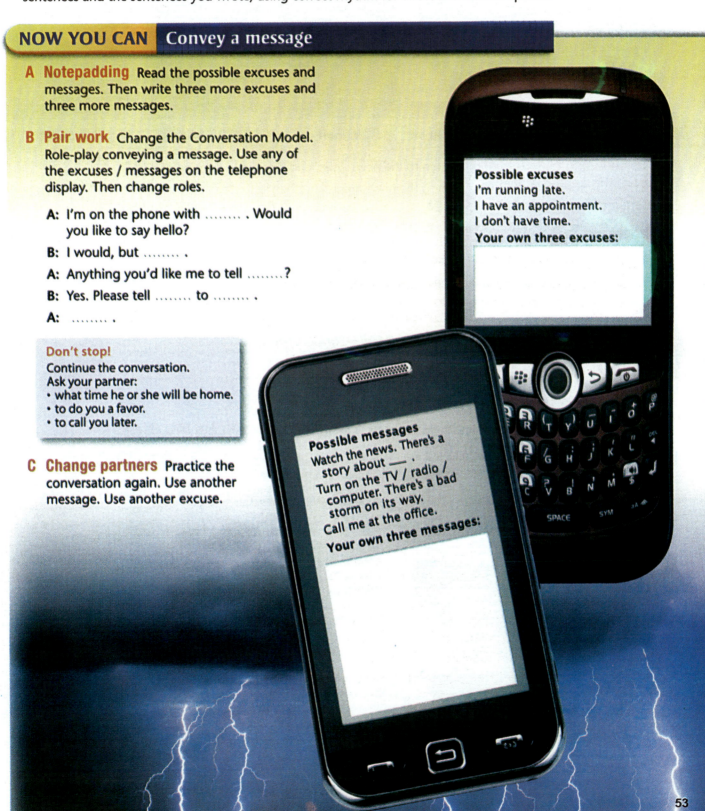

LESSON 2

GOAL Report news

VOCABULARY Severe weather and other natural disasters

A 🔊 3:06 Read and listen. Then listen again and repeat.

a tornado   a hurricane / typhoon   a flood   a landslide   a drought

B 🔊 3:07 **Listening comprehension** Listen to the news. Infer, and then write the kind of event the report describes.

1 ....   3 ....
2 ....   4 ....

C 🔊 3:08 Listen again. After each report, say if the statement is true or false.

1 She said it hadn't rained in a month.   3 She said the storm had done a lot of damage.
2 He said it hadn't rained for a week.   4 He said the storm won't do a lot of damage.

GRAMMAR Indirect speech: <u>say</u> and <u>tell</u>—tense changes

Use <u>tell</u> when you mention the listener. Use <u>say</u> when you don't.
Maggie **told her parents** to stay home. (listeners mentioned)
Maggie **said** to stay home. (listeners not mentioned)

When <u>say</u> and <u>tell</u> are in the past tense, the verbs in the indirect speech statement often change. Present becomes past. Past becomes past perfect.
They said, "The weather **is** awful." → They said (that) the weather **was** awful.
Dan said, "We all **had** the flu." → Dan said (that) they all **had had** the flu.

GRAMMAR BOOSTER • p. 129
• Indirect speech: optional tense changes

A **Grammar practice** Circle the correct verbs for indirect speech.

My Great Grandmother Meets Hurricane Cleo
Hurricane Cleo struck the United States in August, 1964. My great grandmother, Ana, was traveling in Miami when the hurricane struck. She (1 said / told) me that she still remembers how scared everyone was.
She (2 said / told) me that the hotel (3 has called / had called) her room one morning and had (4 said / told) her that a big storm (5 is / was) on its way. They (6 said / told) that all hotel guests (7 have to / had to) stay in the hotel until the weather service (8 tell / said) that it (9 is / was) safe to leave.
She stayed in her room and she didn't know what happened until the storm was over. When she turned on the TV, the reports (10 said / told) that a lot of people (11 have been / had been) injured and that all the roads (12 are / were) flooded. She always (13 says / said) that she still (14 feels / felt) lucky to have survived Hurricane Cleo.

54 UNIT 5

B Grammar practice Change each statement from direct speech to indirect speech, changing the verb tense in the indirect speech statement.

1. The TV reporter said, "The landslide is one of the worst in history."

   The TV reporter said the landslide was one of the worst in history.

2. He also said, "It caused the destruction of half the houses in the town."
3. My sister called and said, "There is no electricity because of the hurricane."
4. The newspaper said, "There was a tornado in the central part of the country."
5. The paper said, "The drought of 1999 was the worst natural disaster of the twentieth century."
6. After the great snowstorm in 1888, a New York newspaper reported, "The blizzard of '88 caused more damage than any previous storm."

CONVERSATION MODEL

A 🔊 Read and listen to a conversation about the news.

A: What's going on in the news today?
B: Well, the *Times* says there was a terrible storm in the south.
A: Really?
B: Yes. It says lots of houses were destroyed.
A: What a shame.
B: But there haven't been any deaths.
A: Thank goodness for that.

B 🔊 **Rhythm and intonation** Listen again and repeat. Then practice the Conversation Model with a partner.

NOW YOU CAN Report news

A Notepadding Read each newspaper headline. Then write what it said on a separate sheet of paper, using indirect speech.

The Morning Herald says there was an earthquake in Iran.

B Pair work Use the newspaper headlines to report what each newspaper says. Then change roles and newspaper headlines.

A: What's going on in the news today?
B: Well, ... says ....
A: Really?
B: Yes. It says ....
A: ....

Don't stop!
Discuss all the facts in the headlines. Express your reactions to the news.

♻ **Be sure to recycle this language.**
Oh, no!
What a disaster.
That's enormous / gigantic / huge / horrendous.

C Change partners Practice the conversation again, using a different headline.

Morning Herald
20,000 killed in earthquake in Iran

DAR POST
People flee flooded river valley

MERCURY
Avian influenza epidemic causes record deaths in Indonesia
Doctors urge children and elderly to receive vaccinations

National News
Drought causes severe famine
Thousands die of hunger

Village Times
Severe dust storm hits Kabul suburbs
Extreme damage to cars, buildings

LESSON 3

GOAL Describe natural disasters

BEFORE YOU READ

mild	!
moderate	!!
severe	!!!
deadly	!!!!
catastrophic	!!!!!

A **Vocabulary** • *Adjectives of severity* Read and listen. Then listen again and repeat.

B Warm-up Have you or someone you know experienced a natural disaster? What kind of disaster was it? How severe was it? Tell the class about it.

READING

EARTHQUAKES

Earthquakes are among the deadliest natural disasters, causing the largest numbers of casualties, the highest death tolls, and the greatest destruction. In 1556 in China, the deadliest earthquake in history killed 830,000 people. But many other earthquakes have caused the deaths of more than 100,000 people, and it is not unusual, even in modern times, for an earthquake death toll to reach 20–30,000 people with hundreds of thousands left homeless and with countless injured. The floodwaters of the 2004 tsunami in Sumatra, which killed over 200,000 people, were caused by a catastrophic earthquake.

There are four factors that affect the casualty rate and economic impact of earthquakes: magnitude, location, quality of construction of buildings, and timing.

Magnitude
The magnitude, or strength, of an earthquake is measured on the Richter scale, ranging from 1 to 10, with 10 being the greatest. Earthquakes over 6 on the Richter scale are often deadly, and those over 8 are generally catastrophic, causing terrible damage.

Location
A severe earthquake that is located far from population centers does not cause the same damage as a less severe one that occurs in the middle of a city. As an example, in 1960, the strongest earthquake ever recorded, 9.5 magnitude on the Richter scale, struck in the Pacific Ocean near the Chilean coastline, destroying buildings, killing over 2,000, and injuring another 3,000 in regional cities near the coast. If this quake had struck a city directly, it would have been catastrophic, and hundreds of thousands might have been killed. Similarly, in Alaska, in 1964, a magnitude 9.2 quake hit an area with few people, and the death toll was 117.

Quality of Construction
Modern building construction techniques can lessen the death toll and economic impact of a moderate earthquake that would otherwise cause severe destruction of older-style buildings. In

The 2008 earthquake in Sichuan Province, China, was one of the deadliest earthquakes in recent history.

2010, a terrible earthquake in Port-au-Prince, the capital of Haiti, caused the destruction of a tremendous number of the city's buildings, mostly due to poor construction. In contrast, an even stronger earthquake later that year in Chile caused less destruction because of that country's use of earthquake-resistant construction.

Timing
Finally, the time of occurrence of an earthquake can affect the number of deaths and casualties. Earthquakes that occur in the night, when people are indoors, usually cause a greater death toll than ones that occur when people are outdoors.

Largest Earthquakes in the World Since 1950		
Place	Year	Magnitude
Off the coast of Chile	1960	9.5
Prince William Sound, Alaska, U.S.	1964	9.2
Off the west coast of northern Sumatra	2004	9.1
Kamchatka, Russia	1952	9.0
Chile	2010	8.8
Rat Islands, Alaska, U.S.	1965	8.7
Northern Sumatra, Indonesia	2005	8.6
Assam—Tibet	1950	8.6
Andreanof Islands, Alaska, U.S.	1957	8.6
Southern Sumatra, Indonesia	2007	8.5

Information source: worldbookonline.com

A Paraphrase Rewrite the following statements in your own words, changing the underlined word or phrase.

1 The <u>magnitude</u> of an earthquake is measured by the Richter scale.
2 There are four <u>factors</u> that affect the destructive value of an earthquake.
3 Good construction techniques can <u>lessen</u> the danger to people in buildings affected by an earthquake.
4 Damage is often <u>due to</u> poor construction.
5 If an earthquake occurs near a major <u>population center</u>, more people will be affected.

B Confirm facts Answer the questions, according to the information in the article. Use indirect speech.

1. Where did the deadliest earthquake in history take place?
2. Which earthquake had the highest recorded Richter scale reading?
3. How can location affect the death toll of an earthquake?
4. What else can lessen the destruction and economic impact of an earthquake?

> " The article said the earthquake in 1556 was the deadliest in history. "

On your *ActiveBook* Self-Study Disc:
Extra Reading Comprehension Questions

C Identify cause and effect Discuss how magnitude and timing affect the casualty rate and economic impact of earthquakes. Explain your ideas by putting together information from the article.

NOW YOU CAN Describe natural disasters

A Pair work Partner A, read the fact sheet about the Jamaica hurricane. Partner B, read the fact sheet about the Philippines earthquake. In your own words, tell your partner about the disaster.

> " A hurricane hit Jamaica on September 20. There was a lot of property damage... "

JAMAICA HURRICANE

Date:	September 20
Place:	Port Royal, Jamaica
Event:	hurricane
Property damage:	many houses damaged by wind, flooding, and landslides
Casualties:	hundreds homeless and missing

PHILIPPINES EARTHQUAKE

Date:	September 14
Place:	Manila, Philippines
Event:	earthquake, magnitude 6.7
Property damage:	moderate in newer buildings, severe in older ones
Casualties:	200 deaths, many injuries, some severe and life-threatening

B Notepadding Choose one of the historic disasters from the list. Find information about it on the Internet, at a library, or in a bookstore. (Or choose a disaster you are already familiar with.) Write details about the disaster on your notepad.

Some historic disasters
- The San Francisco earthquake of 1906 (U.S.)
- The Bam earthquake of 2003 (Iran)
- The tsunami of 2004 (Indian Ocean)
- Hurricane Katrina 2005 (New Orleans, U.S.)
- The earthquake of 2010 (Haiti)
- A natural disaster of your choice: _____

Date:
Place:
Event:
Property damage:
Casualties:

C Group work Make a news broadcast or presentation about the disaster you researched (or one of the disasters in A). Describe the natural disaster to your class.

♻ **Be sure to recycle this language.**

Type of disaster	Adjectives	Features
flood	mild	casualties
storm	moderate	injuries
landslide	severe	property damage
earthquake	deadly	death toll
flood	catastrophic	
famine		
epidemic		

Text-mining (optional)
Underline language in the Reading on page 56 to use in the Group Work.
For example:
" ___ was due to... "

LESSON 4

GOAL Prepare for an emergency

BEFORE YOU LISTEN

A 🔊 **Vocabulary • *Emergency preparations and supplies*** Read and listen. Then listen again and repeat.

evacuate   to remove all people from an area that is too dangerous

an emergency   a very dangerous situation that requires immediate action

a power outage   an interruption in the flow of electrical power over a large area

a shelter   a safe place where people may go when the area they live in has been evacuated

a first-aid kit   a small box or package containing supplies to treat minor injuries and illnesses

a flashlight   a portable, battery-operated light

non-perishable food   food that doesn't need refrigeration, such as canned and dried food

A battery-operated flashlight is a must when there is a power outage.

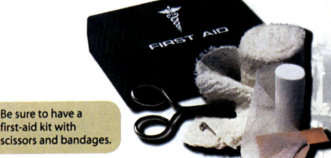

Be sure to have a first-aid kit with scissors and bandages.

B Pair work With a partner, write sentences using the Vocabulary words and phrases.

> They tried to evacuate the entire population of the city before the flood, but lots of people refused to go.

LISTENING COMPREHENSION

A 🔊 **Listen for main ideas** Listen to an emergency radio broadcast. Write a sentence to describe the emergency the broadcaster is reporting.

....

....

B 🔊 **Listen for details** Listen again and correct each of the following false statements, using indirect speech.

Example: He said you should stand near windows during the storm.

> ❝ No. He said <u>not</u> to stand near windows during the storm. ❞

1 He said you should turn your refrigerator and freezer off.

2 He said that in case of a flood, you should put valuable papers on the lowest floor of your home.

3 He said you should read the newspapers for the location of shelters.

C Paraphrase What did the radio announcer say in the emergency radio broadcast? With a partner, discuss the questions and complete each statement in indirect speech. Listen again if necessary.

1. What should you do to get your car ready for an evacuation?
   He said to ....
2. What should you do with outdoor furniture?
   He said to ....
3. What should you buy for flashlights and portable radios?
   He said to ....
4. What should you listen to in case of an evacuation?
   He said to ....
5. How should you prepare to have food and water in case you have to stay indoors for several days?
   He said to ....

NOW YOU CAN Prepare for an emergency

Kinds of emergencies
- a flood
- a tornado
- a severe storm (blizzard, hurricane, typhoon)
- an epidemic
- a famine
- a drought
- a landslide
- an earthquake

A Group work Choose an emergency from the list. Write plans for your emergency on the notepad. Provide a reason for each plan.

Plans	Reasons
Have 2 liters of water per person per day.	to have enough water in case the water is unsafe to drink

Type of emergency:

Plans   Reasons

batteries   matches   bottled water

" Our group prepared for a storm. We said to be sure cell phones were working. A power outage might occur. "

B Present your plans to the class. Compare your plans.

Review

More Practice
ActiveBook *Self-Study Disc*
grammar · vocabulary · listening
reading · speaking · pronunciation

A 🔊 **Listening comprehension** Listen to the report. The reporter describes three kinds of disasters. Listen carefully and check the ones that fall into the categories she describes. Listen again if necessary.

		Disaster	Place	Year	Killed
☐	1	epidemic	worldwide	1917	20,000,000
☐	2	famine	Soviet Union	1932	5,000,000
☐	3	flood	China	1931	3,700,000
☐	4	drought	China	1928	3,000,000
☐	5	epidemic	worldwide	1914	3,000,000
☐	6	epidemic	Soviet Union	1917	2,500,000
☐	7	flood	China	1959	2,000,000
☐	8	epidemic	India	1920	2,000,000
☐	9	famine	Bangladesh	1943	1,900,000
☐	10	epidemic	China	1909	1,500,000

The 10 most deadly natural disasters of the 20th century

Source: CRED (Center for Research on the Epidemiology of Disasters)

3:17/3:18
Top Notch Pop
"Lucky to Be Alive"
Lyrics p. 149

B Complete each statement with the name of the disaster or emergency.

1 In ...., mud and soil cover the houses and can bury entire towns.
2 A widespread event in which many people become sick with the same illness is ....
3 A .... occurs when water from a river enters houses and roads.
4 A storm with high winds and rain is ....
5 When there is no rain for a long period of time, ... is said to occur.
6 In ...., there is not enough food and many people go hungry.

C Complete each indirect statement or question with <u>said</u> or <u>told</u>.

1 They .... me to call the office in the morning.
2 The students .... the test had been very difficult.
3 He .... the storm was awful.
4 Who .... us to get extra batteries?

D On a separate sheet of paper, rewrite the following indirect speech statements in direct speech.

1 She said they knew the reason there was so much property damage.
2 The radio announcer told the people to fill up their cars with gas before the storm.
3 I said not to tell the children about the storm.
4 He asked if the epidemic had been severe.

E On a separate sheet of paper, rewrite the following direct speech statements in indirect speech.

1 Robert told Marie, "Don't wait for the evacuation order."
2 Sylvia said, "I think the earthquake occurred during the night."
3 The emergency broadcast said, "Buy bottled water before the hurricane."
4 They told Marlene, "Call us the next day."

F **Writing** On a separate sheet of paper, write about how to prepare for an emergency. Choose an emergency and include information on what to do, what supplies to have, and what preparations to make.

WRITING BOOSTER ▸ p. 144
• Organizing detail statements by order of importance
• Guidance for Exercise F

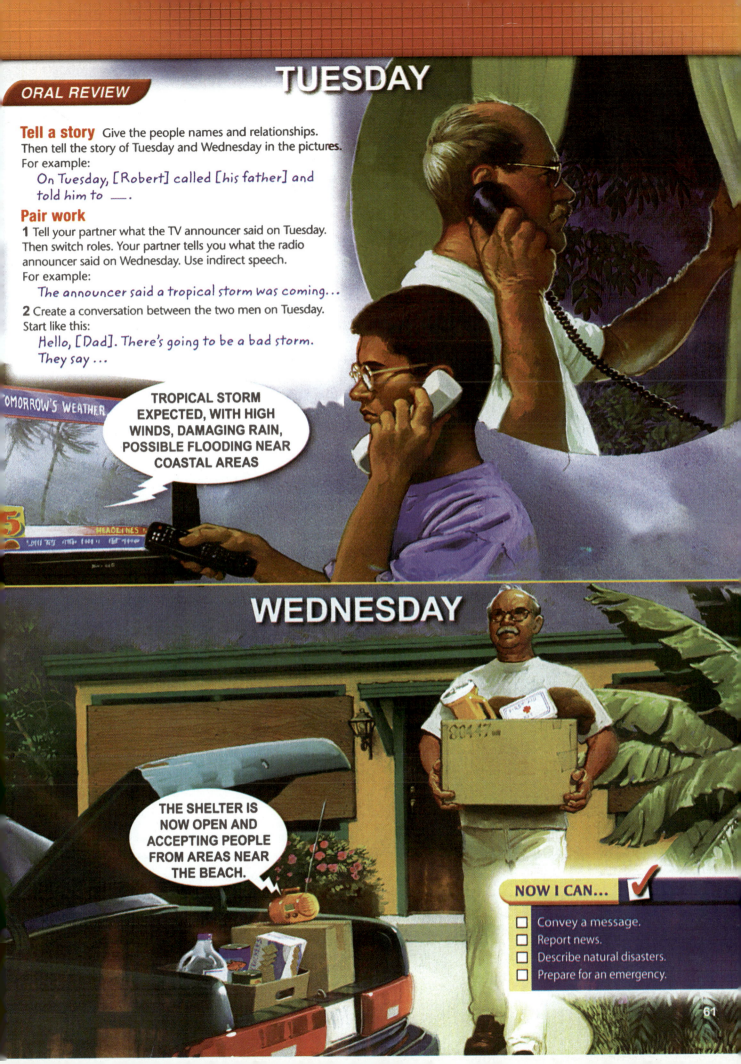

Grammar Booster

The Grammar Booster is optional. It is not required for the achievement tests in the *Top Notch Complete Assessment Package*. If you use the Grammar Booster, there are extra Grammar Booster exercises in the Workbook in a separate labeled section.

UNIT 1 Lesson 1

Tag questions: short answers

Look at the affirmative and negative short answers to the tag questions from page 4.

You're Lee, **aren't you**?	Yes, I am. / No, I'm not.
You're not Amy, **are you**?	Yes, I am. / No, I'm not.
She speaks Thai, **doesn't she**?	Yes, she does. / No, she doesn't.
I don't know you, **do I**?	Yes, you do. / No, you don't.
He's going to drive, **isn't he**?	Yes, he is. / No, he isn't.
We're not going to eat here, **are we**?	Yes, we are. / No, we aren't.
They'll be here later, **won't they**?	Yes, they will. / No, they won't.
It won't be long, **will it**?	Yes, it will. / No, it won't.
You were there, **weren't you**?	Yes, I was. / No, I wasn't.
He wasn't driving, **was he**?	Yes, he was. / No, he wasn't.
They left, **didn't they**?	Yes, they did. / No, they didn't.
We didn't know, **did we**?	Yes, you did. / No, you didn't.
It's been a great day, **hasn't it**?	Yes it has. / No, it hasn't.
She hasn't been here long, **has she**?	Yes, she has. / No she hasn't.
Ann would like Quito, **wouldn't she**?	Yes, she would. / No, she wouldn't.
You wouldn't do that, **would you**?	Yes, I would. / No, I wouldn't.
They can hear me, **can't they**?	Yes, they can. / No, they can't.
He can't speak Japanese, **can he**?	Yes, he can. / No, he can't.

A Complete each conversation by circling the correct tag question and completing the short answer.

1. A: Mary would like to study foreign cultures (would / wouldn't) she?
   B: Yes, _____.

2. A: It's a long time until dinner, (is / isn't) it?
   B: No, _____.

3. A: We met last summer, (did / didn't) we?
   B: Yes, _____.

4. A: They're starting the meeting really late, (haven't / aren't) they?
   B: No, _____.

5. A: There weren't too many delays in the meeting, (wasn't it / were there)?
   B: No, _____.

6. A: You don't know what to do, (do / don't) you?
   B: No, _____.

7. A: There isn't any reason to call, (is / isn't) there?
   B: No, _____.

8. A: It's awful to not have time for lunch, (isn't it / aren't you)?
   B: Yes, _____.

9. A: When you know etiquette, you can feel comfortable anywhere, (can / can't) you?
   B: Yes, _____.

10. A: It's really getting late, (is it / isn't it)?
    B: No, _____.

B Correct the error in each item.

1. They'd both like to study abroad, ~~would~~ *wouldn't* they?
2. It's only a six-month course, is it?
3. Clark met his wife on a rafting trip, didn't Clark?
4. Marian made three trips to Japan last year, hasn't she?
5. There were a lot of English-speaking people on the tour, wasn't it?
6. The students don't know anything about that, don't they?
7. There isn't any problem with my student visa, isn't there?
8. It's always interesting to travel with people from other countries, aren't they?
9. With English, you can travel to most parts of the world, can you?
10. I'm next, don't I?

UNIT 1 Lesson 2

Verb usage: present and past (review)

The simple present tense (but NOT the present continuous):
- for facts and regular occurrences
  I **study** English. Class **meets** every day. Water **boils** at 100°.
- with frequency adverbs and time expressions
  They never **eat** before 6:00 on weekdays.
- with stative ("non-action") verbs
  I **remember** her now.
- for future actions, especially those indicating schedules
  Flight 100 usually leaves at 2:00, but tomorrow it **leaves** at 1:30.

The present continuous (but NOT the simple present tense):
- for actions happening now (but NOT with stative [non-action] verbs)
  They**'re talking** on the phone.
- for actions occurring during a time period in the present
  This year I**'m studying** English.
- for some future actions, especially those already planned
  Thursday I**'m going** to the theater.

The present perfect or the present perfect continuous:
- for unfinished or continuous actions
  I**'ve lived** here since 2007. OR I**'ve been living** here since 2007.
  I**'ve lived** here for five years. OR I**'ve been living** here for five years.

The present perfect (but NOT the present perfect continuous):
- for completed or non-continuing actions
  I**'ve eaten** there three times.
  I**'ve never** read that book.
  I**'ve** already **seen** him.

The simple past tense:
- for actions completed at a specified time in the past
  I **ate** there in 2010. NOT I've eaten there in 2010.

The past continuous:
- for one or more actions in progress at a time in the past
  At 7:00, we **were eating** dinner.
  They **were swimming** and we **were sitting** on the beach.

The past continuous and the simple past tense:
- for an action that interrupted a continuing action in the past
  I **was eating** when my sister **called**.

Use to / used to :
- for past situations and habits that no longer exist
  I **used to smoke**, but I stopped.
  They **didn't use to require** a visa, but now they do.

The past perfect:
- to indicate that one past action preceded another past action
  When I arrived, they **had finished** lunch.

Stative (non-action) verbs

appear	notice
be	own
believe	possess
belong	prefer
contain	remember
cost	see
feel	seem
hate	smell
have	sound
hear	suppose
know	taste
like	think
look	understand
love	want
need	weigh

A Correct the verbs in the following sentences.

1 I talk on the phone with my fiancé right now.
2 She's usually avoiding sweets.
3 They eat dinner now and can't talk on the phone.
4 Every Friday I'm going to the gym at 7:00.
5 Burt is wanting to go home early.
6 Today we all study in the library.
7 The train is never leaving before 8:00.
8 Water is freezing when the temperature goes down.
9 We're liking coffee.
10 On most days I'm staying home.

Grammar Booster

B Complete each sentence with the present perfect continuous.

1 We _____ to this spa for two years.
   (come)
2 *Slumdog Millionaire* _____ at the Classic Cinema since last Saturday.
   (play)
3 Robert _____ for an admissions letter from the language school for a week.
   (wait)
4 The tour operators _____ weather conditions for the rafting trip.
   (worry about)
5 I _____ that tour with everyone.
   (talk about)

C Check the sentences and questions that express unfinished or continuing actions. Then, on a separate sheet of paper, change the verb phrase in those sentences to the present perfect continuous.

The Averys have lived in New York since the late nineties.
The Averys have been living in New York since the late nineties.

☐ 1 Their relatives have already called them.
☐ 2 We have waited to see them for six months.
☐ 3 I haven't seen the Berlin Philharmonic yet.
☐ 4 This is the first time I've visited Dubai.
☐ 5 We have eaten in that old Peruvian restaurant for years.
☐ 6 Has he ever met your father?
☐ 7 How long have they studied Arabic?
☐ 8 My husband still hasn't bought a car.
☐ 9 The kids have just come back from the soccer game.

UNIT 2   Lesson 1

Other ways to draw conclusions: *probably*; *most likely*

Two other ways to draw conclusions are with **probably** and **most likely**. These indicate less certainty than **must**.

Probably frequently occurs after the verb **be** or when **be** is part of a verb phrase.
   They're **probably** at the dentist's office.
   It's **probably** going to rain.

Use **probably** before **isn't** or **aren't**. With **is not** or **are not**, use **probably** before **not**.
   She **probably** isn't feeling well.
   She's **probably** not feeling well.

Use **probably** before other verbs.
   He **probably** forgot about the appointment.
   The dentist **probably** doesn't have time to see a new patient.

Be careful! Don't use **probably** after verbs other than **be**.
Don't say: He ~~forgot probably~~ about the appointment.

You can also use **Probably** or **Most likely** at the beginning of a sentence to draw a conclusion.
   Probably she's a teacher. / **Most likely** she's a teacher.
   Probably he forgot about the appointment. / **Most likely** he forgot about the appointment.

On a separate sheet of paper, rewrite each sentence with **probably** or **most likely**.

1 He must have a terrible cold.
2 She must be feeling very nauseous.
3 They must not like going to the dentist.
4 The dentist must not be in her office today.
5 Acupuncture must be very popular in Asia.
6 A conventional doctor must have to study for a long time.

Grammar Booster

UNIT 2 Lesson 2

Expressing possibility with maybe

Maybe most frequently occurs at the beginning of a sentence.
  Maybe he needs an X-ray. (= He may need an X-ray.)

Be careful! Don't confuse **maybe** and **may be**.
She **may be** a doctor.
NOT She maybe a doctor.
Maybe she's a doctor.
NOT May be she's a doctor.

On a separate sheet of paper, rewrite each sentence with **maybe**.

1 His doctor may use herbal therapy.
2 Conventional medicine may be the best choice.
3 The doctor may want to take a blood test.
4 She may prefer to wait until tomorrow.
5 They may be afraid to see a dentist.

UNIT 3 Lesson 1

Let to indicate permission

Use an object and the base form of a verb with **let**.
  object   base form
She **let** her sister **wear** her favorite skirt.

Be careful!
Don't say: She let her sister to wear her favorite skirt.

Let has the same meaning as **permit**.
Use **let** to indicate that permission is being given to do something.
  My boss **let** me **take** the day off.
  I **don't let** my children **stay** out after 9:00 P.M.
  Why **don't** you **let** me **help** you?

A On a separate sheet of paper, rewrite each sentence, using **let**.

1 Don't permit your younger brother to open the oven door.
2 You should permit your little sister to go to the store with you.
3 We don't permit our daughter to eat a lot of candy.
4 I wouldn't permit my youngest son to go to the mall alone.
5 Why don't you permit your children to see that movie?
6 You should permit them to make their own decision.
7 We always permit him to stay out late.

Causative have: common errors

Be careful! Don't confuse the simple past tense causative **have** with the past perfect auxiliary **have**.
  I **had them call** me before 10:00. (They called me.)
  I **had called** them before 10:00. (I called them.)

B Who did what? Read each sentence. Complete each statement. Follow the example.

We had them fix the car before our trip.	_They_ fixed _the car_.	
We had fixed the car before our trip.	_We_ fixed _the car_.	
1 Janet had already called her mother.	_____ called _____.	
Janet had her mother call the train station.	_____ called _____.	
2 Mark had his friends help him with moving.	_____ helped _____.	
Mark had helped his friends with moving.	_____ helped _____.	
3 My father had signed the check for his boss.	_____ signed _____.	
My father had his boss sign the check.	_____ signed _____.	
4 Mr. Gates had them open the bank early.	_____ opened _____.	
Mr. Gates had opened the bank early.	_____ opened _____.	

Grammar Booster

UNIT 3   Lesson 2

The passive causative: the by phrase

Use a <u>by</u> phrase if knowing who performed the action is important.
  I had my dress shortened **by the tailor** at the shop next to the train station.

If knowing who performed the action is not important, you don't need to include a <u>by</u> phrase.
  I had my dress shortened ~~by someone~~ at the shop next to the train station.

On a separate sheet of paper, use the cues to write advice about services, using <u>you should</u> and the passive causative <u>get</u> or <u>have</u>. Use a <u>by</u> phrase if the information is important. Follow the example.

shoe / repair / Mr. B / at the Boot Stop
You should get your shoes repaired by Mr. B at the Boot Stop.

1 picture / frame / Lydia / at Austin Custom Framing
2 hair / cut / Eva / at the Curl Up Hair Salon
3 photos / print / at the mall
4 a suit / make / Luigi / at Top Notch Tailors
5 sweaters / dry-clean / at Midtown Dry Cleaners

UNIT 4   Lesson 1

Verbs that can be followed by clauses with that

The following verbs often have noun clauses as their direct objects. Notice that each verb expresses a kind of "mental activity." In each case, it is optional to include <u>that</u>.

She	agrees / thinks / believes / feels	(that) the students should work harder.	I	assume / suppose / doubt / guess	(that) they made reservations.
We	hear / see / understand / hope	(that) the government has a new plan.	He	forgot / noticed / realized / remembered / knew	(that) the stores weren't open.
They	decided / discovered / dreamed / hoped / learned	(that) everyone could pass the test.			

Adjectives that can be followed by clauses with that

Use a clause with <u>that</u> after a predicate adjective of emotion to further explain its meaning.

I'm	afraid / angry	(that) we'll have to leave early.	He's	sorry / unhappy	(that) the flight was cancelled.
We're	worried / ashamed	(that) we won't be on time to the event.	She's	surprised / disappointed	(that) the news spread so fast.
They're	happy / sad	(that) the teacher is leaving.			

On a separate sheet of paper, complete each sentence in your own way. Use clauses with <u>that</u>.

1 When I was young, I couldn't believe . . .
2 Last year, I decided . . .
3 This year, I was surprised to discover . . .
4 Last week, I forgot . . .
5 Recently, I heard . . .
6 In the future, I hope . . .
7 Now that I study English, I know . . .
8 In the last year, I learned . . .
9 Not long ago, I remembered . . .
10 Recently, I dreamed . . .
11 (your own idea)
12 (your own idea)

UNIT 4 Lesson 2

Embedded questions: usage and common errors

You can use an embedded question to ask for information more politely.
Are we late? → Can you tell me **if we're late**?
What time is it? → Can you tell me **what time it is**?
Why isn't it working? → Could you explain **why it isn't working**?
Where's the bathroom? → Do you know **where the bathroom is**?
How do I get to the bank? → Would you mind telling me **how I get to the bank**?

Be careful! Do not use the question form in embedded questions.
Do you know **why she won't read** the newspaper?
Don't say: Do you know why ~~won't she~~ read the newspaper?
Can you tell me **if this bus runs** express?
Don't say: Can you tell me ~~does this bus run~~ express?

Phrases that are often followed by embedded questions
I don't know . . .
I'd like to know . . .
Let me know . . .
I can't remember . . .
Let's ask . . .
I wonder . . .
I'm not sure . . .
Do you know . . . ?
Can you tell me . . . ?
Can you remember . . . ?
Could you explain . . . ?
Would you mind telling me . . . ?

Embedded questions: punctuation

Sentences with embedded questions are punctuated according to the meaning of the whole sentence.

If an embedded question is in a sentence, use a period.
I don't know (something)**.** → I don't know **who she is.**

If an embedded question is in a question, use a question mark.
Can you tell me (something)**?** → Can you tell me **who she is?**

A On a separate sheet of paper, complete each sentence with an embedded question. Punctuate each sentence correctly.

1 Please let me know (When does the movie start?)
2 I wonder (Where is the subway station?)
3 Can you tell me (How do you know that?)
4 We're not sure (What should we bring for dinner?)
5 They'd like to understand (Why doesn't Pat want to come to the meeting?)
6 Please tell the class (Who painted this picture?)

B On a separate sheet of paper, rewrite each question more politely, using noun clauses with embedded questions. Begin each one with a different phrase. Follow the example.

Where's the airport? *Can you tell me where the airport is?*

1 What time does the concert start?
2 How does this new MP3 player work?
3 Why is the express train late?
4 Where is the nearest bathroom?
5 Who speaks English at that hotel?
6 When does Flight 18 arrive from Paris?

C Correct the wording and punctuation errors in each item.

1. Could you please tell me does this train go to Nagoya.
2. I was wondering can I get your phone number?
3. I'd like to know what time does the next bus arrive?
4. Can you tell me how much does this magazine cost.
5. Do you remember where did he use to live?
6. I'm not sure why do they keep calling me.
7. I wonder will she come on time?

Embedded questions with infinitives

In embedded questions, an infinitive can be used to express possibility (can or could) or advice (should). You can use an infinitive after the question word. The following sentences have the same meaning.
  I don't know **where I can get** that magazine. = I don't know **where to get** that magazine.
  I'm not sure **when I should call** them. = I'm not sure **when to call** them.
  She wanted to know **which train she should take**. = She wanted to know **which train to take**.

You can also use an infinitive after **whether**.
  I can't decide **whether I should read** this book next. = I can't decide **whether to read** this book next.

Be careful! Don't use an infinitive after **if**. Use **whether** instead.
  I can't decide **if I should read** this book next. = I can't decide **whether to read** this book next.
  Don't say: I can't decide if to read this book next.

D On a separate sheet of paper, rewrite each sentence with an infinitive.

1. Could you tell me whose novel I should read next?
2. I'd like to know where I can buy Smith's latest book.
3. Can you remember who I should call to get that information?
4. I'd like to know which train I can take there.
5. Let me know if I should give her the magazine when I'm done.
6. I wasn't sure when I could get the new edition of her book.
7. Let's ask how we can get to the train station.

Noun clauses as subjects and objects

A noun clause can function as either a subject or an object in a sentence.

As a subject
What he wrote inspired many people.
Where the story takes place is fascinating.
How she became a writer is an interesting story.
That she wrote the novel in six months is amazing.
Who wrote the article isn't clear.

As an object
I like **what he wrote**.
I want to know **where the story takes place**.
They are inspired by **how she became a writer**.
I heard **that she wrote the novel in six months**.
I wonder **who wrote the article**.

E On a separate sheet of paper, use the prompts to write sentences with noun clauses.

1. People always ask me (Why did I decide to study English?)
2. (She wrote science fiction novels.) has always fascinated me.
3. We all wanted to know (Where did she go on vacation?)
4. (What websites do you visit?) is important information for companies who want to sell you their products.
5. Can you tell me (Who did you invite to dinner?)
6. (How did you decide to become a teacher?) is an interesting story.

UNIT 5 Lesson 1

Direct speech: punctuation rules

When writing direct speech, use quotation marks to indicate the words the speaker actually said. Put final punctuation marks before the second quotation mark.
   Jeremy said, "Don't answer the phone."

Use a comma after the verb or verb phrase that introduces the quoted speech.
   They said, "Call me after the storm."

Begin the quoted speech with a capital letter.
   I said, "Please come to dinner at nine."

A On a separate sheet of paper, write and punctuate each of the following statements in direct speech. Follow the example.

They said tell us when you will be home
They said, "Tell us when you will be home."

1 Martin told me don't get a flu shot
2 My daughter said please pick me up after school
3 The English teacher said read the newspaper tonight and bring in a story about the weather
4 We said please don't forget to listen to the news
5 They said don't buy milk
6 We told them please call us in the morning
7 She said please tell your parents I'm sorry I can't talk right now

B Look at each statement in indirect speech. Then on a separate sheet of paper, complete each statement. Using the prompt, make the indirect speech statement a direct speech statement. Use correct punctuation.

1 They told us to be home before midnight. (They told us)
2 The sign downtown said to pack emergency supplies before the storm. (The sign downtown said)
3 Your daughter called and told me to turn on the radio and listen to the news about the flood. (Your daughter told me)
4 Your parents said not to call them before 9 A.M. (Your parents said)
5 Mr. Rossi phoned to tell me not to go downtown this afternoon. (Mr. Rossi phoned to tell me)

UNIT 5 Lesson 2

Indirect speech: optional tense changes

When the reporting verbs <u>say</u> or <u>tell</u> are in the simple past tense, it is not always necessary to use a different tense in indirect speech from the one the speaker used. The following are three times when it's optional:

When the statement refers to something JUST said:
   I just heard the news. They said a storm **is** coming.
   OR I just heard the news. They said a storm **was** coming.

When the quoted speech refers to something that's still true:
   May told us she **wants** to get a flu shot tomorrow.
   OR May told us she **wanted** to get a flu shot tomorrow.

When the quoted speech refers to a scientific or general truth:
   They said that English **is** an international language.
   OR They said that English **was** an international language.

Be careful! Remember that when the reporting verb is in the present tense, the verb tense in indirect speech does not change.
   They **say** a big storm **is** expected to arrive tomorrow morning.
   Don't say: They say a big storm ~~was~~ …

On a separate sheet of paper, write each direct speech statement in indirect speech. Change the verb in the indirect speech only if necessary.

1 Last Friday my husband said, "I'm going to pick up some things at the pharmacy before the storm."
2 Last year my parents said, "We're going to Spain on vacation this year."
3 She told them, "This year's flu shot is not entirely protective against the flu."
4 He just said, "The danger of a flood is over."
5 We always say, "It's easier to take the train than drive."
6 When I was a child, my parents told me, "It's really important to get a good education."
7 The National Weather Service is saying, "Tonight's weather is terrible."
8 Your parents just told me, "We want to leave for the shelter immediately."

Grammar Booster

Writing Booster

The Writing Booster is optional. It is intended to orient students to the elements of good writing. Each unit's Writing Booster is focused both on a skill and its application to the Writing topic from the Review page.

UNIT 1 Formal e-mail etiquette

Social e-mails between friends are informal and have almost no rules. Friends don't mind seeing spelling or grammar errors and use "emoticons" and abbreviations.

Emoticons	Abbreviations
☺ = I'm smiling.	LOL = "Laughing out loud"
☹ = I'm not happy.	LMK = "Let me know"
	BTW = "By the way"
	IMHO = "In my humble opinion"

However, because e-mail is so fast and convenient, it is commonly used in business communication and between people who have a more formal relationship. When writing a more formal e-mail, it is not acceptable to use the same informal style you would use when communicating with a friend.

For formal e-mails...

Do:
- Use title and last name and a colon in the salutation, unless you are already on a first-name basis:
  Dear Mr. Samuelson:
  Dear Dr. Kent:
  If you are on a first-name basis, it's appropriate to address the person with his or her first name:
  Dear Marian:
- Write in complete sentences, not fragments or run-on sentences.
- Check and correct your spelling.
- Use capital and lowercase letters correctly.
- Use correct punctuation.
- Use a complimentary close as in a formal letter, such as:
  Sincerely, Cordially, Thank you, Thanks so much.
- End with your name, even though it's already in the e-mail message bar.

Don't:
- Use emoticons.
- Use abbreviations such as "LOL" or "u" for "you."
- Use all lowercase letters.
- Date the e-mail the way you would a written letter. (The date is already in the headings bar.)

A Circle all the formal e-mail etiquette errors in the following e-mail to a business associate. Then explain your reasons.

Glenn, it was nice to see u yesterday at the meeting. I was wondering if we could continue the meeting sometime next week. Maybe on Tuesday at your place? There's still a lot we need 2 discus. I know you love long meetings LMK if u wanna change the time.

B Guidance for Writing (page 12) Use the do's and don'ts to check the two e-mail messages you wrote for Exercise D.

UNIT 2 Comparisons and contrasts

COMPARISONS: Use this language to compare two things:

To introduce similarities
- **be alike**
  Herbal medicine and homeopathy **are alike** in some ways.
- **be similar to**
  Homeopathy **is similar to** conventional medicine in some ways.

To provide details
- **both**
  Both herbal medicine and homeopathy are based on plants. / Herbal medicine and homeopathy are **both** based on plants.
- **and ... too**
  Herbal medicine is based on plants **and** homeopathy is **too**.
- **and ... (not) either**
  Herbal medicine doesn't use medications **and** homeopathy **doesn't either**.
- **also**
  Many of the medications in conventional medicine **also** come from plants.
- **as well**
  Many of the medications in conventional medicine come from plants **as well**.
- **Likewise,**
  Herbs offer an alternative to conventional medications. **Likewise**, homeopathy offers a different approach.
- **Similarly,**
  Similarly, homeopathy offers a different approach.

CONTRASTS: Use this language to contrast two things:

To introduce differences
- **be different from**
  Conventional medicine **is different from** acupuncture in a number of ways.

To provide details
- **but**
  Herbal medicine treats illness with herbs, **but** acupuncture mainly treats illness with needles.
- **while / whereas**
  Herbal medicine treats illness with herbs **while** (or **whereas**) acupuncture treats illness with needles. OR **While** (or **Whereas**) herbal medicine treats illness with herbs, acupuncture treats illness with needles.
- **unlike**
  Spiritual healing involves taking responsibility for one's own healing, **unlike** conventional medicine. OR **Unlike** conventional medicine, spiritual healing involves taking responsibility for one's own healing.
- **However,**
  Conventional doctors routinely treat heart disease with bypass surgery. **However,** acupuncturists take a different approach.
- **In contrast,**
  Herbal doctors treat illnesses with teas made from plants. **In contrast,** conventional doctors use medicines and surgery.
- **On the other hand,**
  Conventional medicine is based on modern scientific research. **On the other hand,** herbal therapy is based on centuries of common knowledge.

A On a separate sheet of paper, make comparisons, using the cues in parentheses.

1. There's nothing scarier than having a toothache while traveling. Feeling short of breath while on the road can be a frightening experience. (likewise)
2. Many painkillers can be bought without a prescription. Many antihistamines can be bought without a prescription. (both)
3. A broken tooth requires a visit to the dentist. A lost filling requires a visit to the dentist. (and . . . too)
4. You may have to wait for the results of an X-ray. The results of a blood test may not be ready for several days. (similarly)
5. An X-ray doesn't take much time to do. A blood test doesn't take much time to do. (and… not / either)

B On a separate sheet of paper, make contrasts, using the cues in parentheses.

1. If you feel pain in your back, you can try taking a painkiller. If you have pain in your chest, you should see a doctor. (on the other hand)
2. Homeopathy is fairly common in Europe. It is not as popular in the United States. (while)
3. Spiritual healing uses the mind or religious faith to treat illnesses. Other types of treatments do not. (unlike)
4. Conventional medicine and acupuncture have been used for thousands of years. Homeopathy was only introduced in the late 18th century. (whereas)
5. Many people choose conventional medicine first when they need medical help. About 80% of the world's population uses some form of herbal therapy for their regular health care. (however)

C **Guidance for Writing (page 24)** On a separate sheet of paper, write three statements that show similarities in the two medical treatments you chose to write about in Exercise E and three statements that contrast them. Use the language of comparison and contrast in each statement. Use these statements in your writing.

UNIT 3 Supporting an opinion with personal examples

Use these expressions to state your opinions. Follow the punctuation style in the examples.

- **In my opinion,**
  In my opinion, there's nothing wrong with being a procrastinator. People just have different personalities.
- **To me,**
  To me, it's better to be well-organized. Being a procrastinator keeps a person from getting things done.
- **From my point of view,**
  From my point of view, if you aren't well-organized, you're going to have a lot of problems in life.
- **I believe**
  I believe that people who are procrastinators have other strengths such as creativity.
- **I find**
  I find being well-organized helps a person get more done.

Note: All of these expressions can be used either at the beginning of a sentence or at the end. Use a comma before the expression when you use it at the end of a sentence.
There's nothing wrong with being a procrastinator, **in my opinion**.
Being well-organized helps a person get more done, **I find**.

Writing Booster

Use personal examples to make your opinions clear and interesting to readers.

- **For example,**
  I'm usually on time in everything I do. **For example,** I always pay my bills on time.
- **For instance,**
  My brother is usually on time in everything he does, but sometimes he isn't. **For instance,** last week he completely forgot to get our mother a birthday gift.
- **…, such as …**
  There are a few things I tend to put off, **such as** paying bills and studying for tests.
- **Whenever**
  Some people have a hard time paying their bills on time. **Whenever** my husband receives a bill, he puts it on the shelf and forgets about it.
- **Every time**
  Every time I forget to pay a bill, I feel terrible.
- **When I was …**
  I had to learn how to be well-organized. **When I was** a child, my parents did everything for me.

> **Be careful!**
> Do not use for example or for instance to combine sentences.
> Don't write: I'm usually on time for everything I do, for example, I always pay my bills on time.

> **Remember:**
> Use a comma before such as when it introduces a dependent clause.

A On a separate sheet of paper, write a sentence expressing your personal opinion in response to each of the following questions.

1. Do you think children should study the arts in school?
2. Do you think extroverts are better people than introverts?
3. Do you think it's OK to wear casual clothes in an office?

B On a separate sheet of paper, provide a personal example for each of the following statements.

1. I'm (I'm not) a very well-organized person.
2. Some (None) of the people I know procrastinate.
3. I always (don't always) pay my bills on time.
4. I've always (never) had a hard time doing things on time.

C **Guidance for Writing (page 36)** On a separate sheet of paper, state your opinion on the topic in Exercise D. Then list at least five personal examples to support your view. Use the examples in your writing.

UNIT 4 *Summarizing*

A good summary provides only the main ideas of a much longer reading, movie, or event. It should not include lots of details. Here are two effective ways to write a summary:

1. **Answer basic information questions:** For a longer reading, one approach to writing a summary is to think about the answers to basic questions of: Who?, What?, When?, Where?, Why?, and How?
2. **Focus on main ideas instead of details:** For a shorter reading, identify the main ideas. Sentences that are main ideas provide enough information to tell the story. After you have identified the sentences that express the main ideas, rewrite them in your own words.

> **Some basic information questions:**
>
> **Who was the book about?**
> The book I read is about Benito Juárez.
> **Who was Juárez?**
> Juárez was the president of Mexico from 1867 to 1872.
> **Why was he important?**
> He restored the Republic and modernized the country.

A Practice answering basic information questions. Think of a movie you really like. On a separate sheet of paper, write any answers you can to the following questions.

1. Who is the movie about?
2. When does the movie take place?
3. Where does the movie take place?
4. In three to five sentences, what is the movie about?
5. What actors are in the movie? Who is the director?
6. (Add your own information question)

Writing Booster

B Practice focusing on main ideas. In the following article, underline any sentences you think are main ideas. Cross out any sentences that you think are details.

Thirty years ago, most people in the United States, Canada, and Europe didn't think about what to wear to work in an office. Men always wore suits and ties. Women wore suits or conservative skirt outfits. But in the 1990's, that started to change.

It began with "casual Fridays." During the summer, some companies invited their employees to "dress down," or wear more casual clothes to work on Fridays. The policy quickly became popular with employees. After this, it didn't take long for employees to start dressing more casually every day of the week.

Many employees welcomed the new dress policy and the more comfortable work environment that came with it. Etiquette had definitely changed, and suits and ties were rarely seen in many offices. Some employees went as far as wearing jeans, T-shirts, and sneakers to the office.

Then some people began to change their minds about casual dress at work. Many managers felt that casual dress had led to casual attitudes toward work. Now the etiquette for dress in many companies is beginning to change back again.

After you have completed Exercise B, read this summary of the article. How does it compare with the sentences you underlined in the article?

Thirty years ago, most people in the United States, Canada, and Europe didn't think about what to wear to work in an office. But in the 1990's, that started to change. During the summer, some companies invited their employees to "dress down," or wear more casual clothes to work on Fridays. Then some people began to change their minds about casual dress at work. Now the etiquette for dress in many companies is beginning to change back again.

C Guidance for Writing (page 48) Answer each question if you can. If you cannot answer a question, answer the next one. Then use your answers to write the summary within your review.

1. What is the title of the reading material you chose?
2. Who is the writer?
3. Who is it about?
4. What is it about?
5. Where does it take place?
6. When does it take place?
7. Why was it written?
8. Why is it important?
9. Did you like it? Why or why not?
10. Would you recommend it to others? Why or why not?

UNIT 5 *Organizing detail statements by order of importance*

One way to organize supporting details within a paragraph is by **order of importance**, usually beginning with the most important and ending with the least important. Or, if you wish, it is possible to reverse the order, beginning with the least important and building to the most important.

Imagine you are writing an essay about how to prepare for a trip. Use words and expressions that indicate the relative importance of details to the reader.

First, [or **First and most important,**] make sure your passport is up-to-date. Nothing can be worse than arriving at the airport and not being able to get on the plane.

Second, [or **Next,** or **Following that,**] check the weather for your destination. This will ensure that you bring the right clothes. It's terrible to arrive somewhere and find out that the weather is unusually cold for this time of year. The last thing you want to do is to have to go shopping!

Last, [or **Finally,**] write a list of important phone numbers and e-mail addresses of people you have to contact. It can be hard to get that information if you are out of your own country.

Following are two ways to construct the paragraph:

1. Write a topic sentence stating the main idea of the paragraph and then begin describing the details in order of importance.
   The severity of an earthquake is determined by several factors. **First and most important** is the magnitude of the quake. Really strong earthquakes cause lots of damage, even to well-constructed buildings, no matter where or when they occur. Earthquakes with a Richter reading of 9 or over are uniformly catastrophic. **The second most important factor** is location, …etc.

2. Write a topic sentence that states the details in the order of importance.
   The severity of an earthquake is determined by four factors, in order of importance: magnitude, location, quality of construction, and timing. The magnitude of an earthquake is by far the most significant factor in its destructive power… etc.

Writing Booster

A On a separate sheet of paper, rewrite the following paragraph, inserting words to indicate the relative importance of each item.

> Here are some things not to forget when preparing for an emergency. Call your relatives who live in other places, telling them where you are so they don't worry. Have a discussion with all family members about the importance of listening to emergency broadcasts. Keep a supply of blankets and warm jackets in case of power outages or flooding. Be sure to follow all emergency instructions carefully: your life and the life of your family could depend on it.

Type of emergency: _____

Supplies and resources	Notes
non-perishable food:	
bottled water	
batteries	
cell phones	
smart phones	
GPS devices	
medications	
phone numbers	

B **Guidance for Writing (page 60)** Look at the list of supplies and resources. Number them in order of their importance for the emergency you chose. Write notes about why each one is important. Use your notes to help you write about how to prepare for your emergency.

74 *Writing Booster*

Top Notch Pop Lyrics

It's a Great Day for Love [Unit 1]

Wherever you go,
there are things you should know,
so be aware
of the customs and views—
all the do's and taboos—
of people there.
You were just a stranger in a sea of new faces.
Now we're making small talk on a
first-name basis.

(CHORUS)
It's a great day for love, isn't it?
Aren't you the one I was hoping to find?
It's a great day for love, isn't it?
By the time you said hello,
I had already made up my mind.

Wherever you stay
be sure to obey
the golden rules,
and before you relax,
brush up on the facts
you learned in school.
Try to be polite and always be sure to get
some friendly advice on proper etiquette.

(CHORUS)

And when you smiled at me
and I fell in love,
the sun had just appeared
in the sky above.
You know how much I care, don't you?
And you'll always be there, won't you?

(CHORUS)

X-ray of My Heart [Unit 2]

Thanks for fitting me in.
This heart is killing me.
Oh, that must hurt.
Are you in a lot of pain?
Yes, I thought I'd better
see someone right away.
It might be an emergency—
could you try to explain?

(CHORUS)
Give me something to keep me
from falling apart.
Doctor, won't you please
take an x-ray of my heart.

You know, I'm here on business,
and today I saw a guy ...
Why don't you have a seat
while I do some simple tests?
Thanks. As I was saying,
he walked by without a word.
So that's what's bothering you—
just go home and get some rest!

(CHORUS)

The minute that I saw him
I felt weak in the knees.
Are you dizzy, short of breath?
Does it hurt when you sneeze?
Yes, I have all those symptoms—
and a pain in my chest.
Well, love at first sight
can have painful side effects.
Now, I might not be able
to go to work today.
Could I get a prescription
for some kind of medicine?
Well, let's have a look now.
You might have to heal yourself,
or try another treatment
for the kind of pain you're in.

(CHORUS)

I'll Get Back to You [Unit 3]

Your camera isn't working right.
It needs a few repairs.
You make me ship it overnight.
Nothing else compares.
You had to lengthen your new skirt,
and now you want to get
someone to wash your fancy shirts
and dry them when they're wet.
Come a little closer—
let me whisper in your ear.
Is my message getting across
to you loud and clear?

(CHORUS)
You're always making plans.
I'll tell you what I'll do:
let me think it over and
I'll get back to you.

You want to get your suit dry-cleaned.
You want to get someone
to shorten your new pair of jeans
and call you when they're done.
I guess I'll have them print a sign
and hang it on your shelf,
with four small words in one big line:
"Just do it yourself."
Let me tell you what this song
is really all about.
I'm getting tired of waiting while you
figure it out.
I've heard all your demands,
but I have a life, too.
Let me think it over and
I'll get back to you.
I'm really reliable,
incredibly fast,
extremely helpful
from first to last.
Let me see what I can do.
Day after day,
everybody knows
I always do what I say.

(CHORUS)

A True Life Story [Unit 4]

The story of our lives
is a real page-turner,
and we both know
what it's all about.
It's a fast read,
but I'm a slow learner,
and I want to see
how it all turns out.

(CHORUS)
It's a true life story.
I can't put it down.
If you want to know who's in it,
just look around.

The story of our lives
is a real cliffhanger.
It's hard to follow,
but boy, does it pack a thrill—
a rollercoaster ride
of love and anger,
and if you don't write it,
baby, then I will.

(CHORUS)

You can't judge a book by its cover.
I wonder what you're going to discover.
When you read between the lines,
you never know what you might find.
It's not a poem or a romance novel.
It's not a memoir or a self-help book.
If that's what you like, baby, please
don't bother.
If you want the truth, take another look.

(CHORUS)

Lucky to Be Alive [Unit 5]

(CHORUS)
Thank you for helping me to survive.
I'm really lucky to be alive.

When I was caught in a freezing snowstorm,
you taught me how to stay warm.
When I was running from a landslide
with no place to hide,
you protected me from injury.
Even the world's biggest tsunami
has got nothing on me,
because you can go faster.
You keep me safe from disaster.
You're like some kind of hero—
you're the best friend that I know.

(CHORUS)

When the big flood came with the
pouring rain,
they were saying that a natural
disaster loomed.
You just opened your umbrella.
You were the only fellow who kept calm
and prepared.
You found us shelter.
I never felt like anybody cared
the way that you did when you said,
"I will always be there—
you can bet your life on it."
And when the cyclone turned the day
into night,
you held a flashlight and showed me the safe
way home.

You called for help on your cell phone.
You said you'd never leave me.
You said, "Believe me,
in times of trouble you will never be alone."
They said it wasn't such a bad situation.
It was beyond imagination.
I'm just glad to be alive—
and that is no exaggeration.

(CHORUS)

SECOND EDITION

TOP NOTCH

3A

Workbook

Joan Saslow • Allen Ascher

With Julie C. Rouse

PEARSON

Longman

UNIT 1

Make Small Talk

Preview

1 Read the tips on business etiquette. Then read the situations below. Decide if the behavior in each situation is appropriate or inappropriate.

TIPS ON BUSINESS ETIQUETTE

- Always introduce the most important person first.
- Use your business card as a way to stay in touch with people you meet. Exchanging and saving business cards can help you "network" later.
- Being on time is absolutely necessary for business appointments. The rule is to arrive ten to fifteen minutes early. However, for social events, such as business parties, it is considered impolite to arrive early.
- In major cities, business clothing is usually formal. Blue, black, or gray suits are conservative and always appropriate. In warm climates, neat and comfortable khakis, jeans, or slacks, sometimes with a jacket, are OK. However, the first time you visit a company, it is always best to start with a conservative look.
- Business conversations often take place during meals. The meals are a time to relax, get to know the other person socially, and then talk a little business. Depending on the person's schedule, these meetings can be at breakfast, lunch, or dinner.
- Eye contact is very important. Always look at everyone in your conversation group. Move your eyes from one person to another. It makes people feel important and holds their attention.

SOURCE: www.cyborlink.com

1. While you're meeting with a client, the CEO of your company comes into your office. You introduce the CEO to your client first. ☐ appropriate ☐ inappropriate

2. You are meeting with a group of four people. While speaking, you're looking only at the highest level manager in the group. ☐ appropriate ☐ inappropriate

3. You have an interview at a new company on Friday. You know the company allows employees to dress casually on Fridays, so you decide to wear casual clothing. ☐ appropriate ☐ inappropriate

4. You don't have time during the regular business hours to meet with a client. You decide to meet over dinner. ☐ appropriate ☐ inappropriate

5. You're invited to a business party and the invitation says the party is from 7:00 to 9:00 P.M. You arrive at 6:45. ☐ appropriate ☐ inappropriate

2 Match the correct response to each statement or question. Write the letter on the line.

1. Nice to meet you. _____
2. What is the custom here? _____
3. How would you like to be called? _____
4. Are most people on a first-name basis? _____
5. Nice to meet you, Mr. Reston.

a. Not really. People tend to be more formal here.
b. Please call me by my nickname.
c. Nice to meet you, too.
d. No need to be so formal. Please call me Robert.
e. I'm not sure. It's probably best to watch what others do.

3 WHAT ABOUT YOU? Answer the questions in your own way.

1. What do you prefer to be called by your family? _____
2. What do you like to be called by your friends? _____
3. What do you prefer to be called by your colleagues or classmates? _____

LESSON 1

4 Put the conversation in the correct order. Write the number on the line.

_____ Hi! It's a great day, isn't it?
_____ Nice to meet you, too. Would it be rude to call you Joe?
_____ It really is. Allow me to introduce myself. I'm Amanda Decker.
_____ Absolutely not. Please do.
_____ Great. And call me Amanda.
_____ I'm Joe Hanson. It's nice to meet you.

5 Complete each statement with a tag question.

1. He didn't know about that custom, _____?
2. It's a great day to go to the beach, _____?
3. You learned Japanese in school, _____?
4. Mike will be here later, _____?
5. You're not from Turkey, _____?
6. The program in Bali wasn't very successful, _____?
7. I'm presenting my report at 2, _____?
8. There weren't a lot of people at the conference, _____?

6 Read the situations and complete the tag questions.

1. You think your friend got a good grade on her science test.
   "She ____got____ a good grade on her science test, ____didn't she____?"

2. You see two people talking, but you don't think that they know each other.
   "They ____don't know____ each other, ____do they____?"

3. You're talking to your friend. You think he'll be late to the party tonight.
   "You _____ late to the party tonight, _____?"

4. When you get to class, you think your friend Diane hasn't gotten there yet.
   "Diane _____ here yet, _____?"

5. You heard that your friend Bill was in a car accident yesterday, but you don't think that's true.
   "Bill _____ in a car accident yesterday, _____?"

6. You think that Dr. Jenkins doesn't like to be called by her first name.
   "Dr. Jenkins _____ to be called Kate, _____?"

7 Read the information about Allison McFarland. Then use the information on the form to write statements with tag questions.

Name:	Allison McFarland
Preferred title:	Ms.
Date of birth:	October 27, 1985
Place of birth:	Hong Kong
Country of residence:	Canada
Occupation:	student

1. You're Allison McFarland, aren't you?
2. _____
3. _____
4. _____
5. _____

8 WHAT ABOUT YOU? Which topics are appropriate for small talk in your country? Check <u>yes</u> or <u>no</u>. If you check <u>no</u>, then explain why the topic is not appropriate.

	yes	no	
1. what someone would like to be called	☐	☐	_____
2. how much money a person makes	☐	☐	_____
3. a person's work or studies	☐	☐	_____
4. someone's marital status	☐	☐	_____

Make Small Talk

LESSON 2

9 Look at Ken Klein's weekly planner. Then circle the letter of the answer that completes each sentence. Today is Sunday.

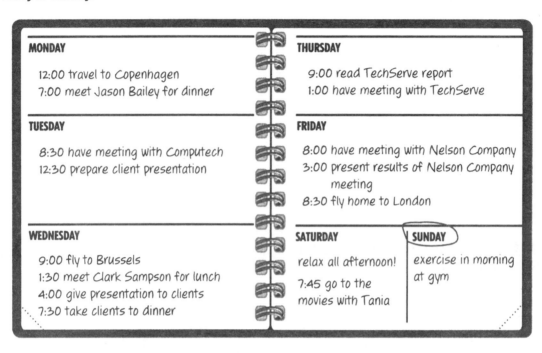

1. By 5:00 P.M. on Monday, Ken _____ to Copenhagen.
   a. had already traveled   b. hadn't yet traveled

2. On Tuesday, Ken _____ Clark Sampson for lunch.
   a. had already met   b. hadn't yet met

3. On Wednesday evening, Ken _____ to Brussels.
   a. hadn't yet flown   b. had already flown

4. Ken _____ the results of the Nelson Company meeting at 2:00 on Friday.
   a. hadn't yet presented   b. had already presented

5. Ken _____ all week before he was able to relax on Saturday.
   a. had worked   b. hadn't worked

10 Look at Ken Klein's weekly planner again. Complete the statements using the past perfect and <u>already</u> or <u>not yet</u>.

1. By the time he flew to Brussels, Ken _had already had_ the meeting with Computech, but he _hadn't yet had_ the meeting with TechServe.

2. At 7:00 P.M. on Wednesday, he _____ the presentation to the clients, but he _____ the clients to dinner.

3. Ken _____ the TechServe report when he had the meeting with TechServe.

4. Ken _____ the meeting with Nelson Company when he had the meeting with TechServe.

5. By Saturday evening, Ken _____ at the gym.

6. At 8:00 on Saturday, Ken _____ to the movies with Tania.

11 Read the Conversation Model on page 7 in the Student's Book again. Then read each sentence below. Circle the letter of the sentence that has the same or similar meaning.

1. "By 9:00 I had already bought my books."
   a. I bought my books before 9:00.
   b. I bought my books at 9:00.

2. "What did you do about lunch?"
   a. Did you have lunch?
   b. Do you want lunch?

3. "When I got to class, I hadn't eaten yet."
   a. I got to class after I ate.
   b. I got to class before I ate.

4. "You must be pretty hungry."
   a. I think you're hungry now.
   b. I'm sure you're hungry now.

12 WHAT ABOUT YOU? Complete the sentences in your own way.

1. When I left the house this morning, I had already _____.

2. At 8:00 today, I hadn't yet _____.

3. By the time I started to study English, I had already _____, but I hadn't yet _____.

LESSON 3

13 Cross out the word or phrase that has a different meaning from the others.

1. offensive   very rude   ~~polite~~
2. customary   not allowed   taboo
3. impolite   nice   rude
4. not usual   traditional   customary
5. etiquette   punctuality   manners

Did you know...

that etiquette and rules for behavior have a very long history? The first instructions for etiquette were written in the year 2400 B.C.E by an Egyptian named Ptahhotep. His guide included advice about how to get along with others and how to advance in the world.

SOURCE: www.canoe.ca

14 Read the article about punctuality. Then read the statements on page 6 and check true, false, or no information, according to the article.

RIGHT ON TIME

Everyone knows that different cultures have different ideas about punctuality. But one country—Ecuador—is trying something new.

A group called Citizens' Participation has found that being late costs the country about $724 million each year. They report that more than half of all public events, as well as many government appointments and social activities, begin late. The group is trying to make people aware of punctuality and is reminding them to be on time. The government, including the Ecuadorian president, is supporting the effort.

Hundreds of Ecuadorian organizations and companies have signed agreements to be on time. Posters have been put up that remind people: "If you're late, someone else is waiting." One newspaper prints a list of government officials who arrive to events late.

The campaign has generally been well-received by the Ecuadorian people, and it seems to be working. Many businesses have reported that more meetings are now beginning on time.

INFORMATION SOURCE: www.economist.com

	true	false	no information
1. The country of Ecuador made more money because people were often late.	☐	☐	☐
2. Citizens' Participation doesn't think punctuality is very important.	☐	☐	☐
3. The government of Ecuador wants people to be on time.	☐	☐	☐
4. Signs and posters have been made to remind people to be punctual.	☐	☐	☐
5. Punctuality is more important now in Ecuador than in most other countries.	☐	☐	☐
6. Ecuadorians are on time less often than they used to be.	☐	☐	☐

15 WHAT ABOUT YOU? How important is punctuality to <u>you</u> for each of the following events? Explain your answers.

	Very important	Somewhat important	Not important	Why?
work or school				
dinner at a friend's house				
a meeting with a co-worker				
a doctor's appointment				
a movie				

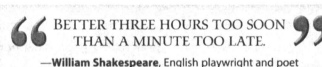

" BETTER THREE HOURS TOO SOON THAN A MINUTE TOO LATE. "
—**William Shakespeare**, English playwright and poet

LESSON 4

16 Extra reading comprehension

Read the article *Formal Dinner Etiquette* on page 10 in the Student's Book again. Check the behavior that would be considered rude at a dinner party in the 1940s. Then write the correct behavior.

1. ☐ You arrive five to ten minutes after the hour set for the dinner.

2. ☐ You arrive late and dinner has started, so you take your seat as quickly as possible and start eating.

3. ☐ If you are a man, you enter the dining room after the women.

4. ☐ You take the seat at the table that your hostess has planned for you.

5. ☐ You start to eat as soon as the food is served to you so that it is still hot when you eat it.

6. ☐ If you are the hostess, you should leave the table as soon as you're done eating.

7. ☐ You leave immediately after the dinner is over.

17 Read the article and then circle the letter of the answer that best completes each sentence.

→ Dressing for Work

HOW CASUAL IS TOO CASUAL?

Thirty years ago or so, most people in the United States, Canada, and Europe didn't think about what to wear to work in an office. Men always wore suits and ties. Women wore suits or conservative skirt outfits. But in the 1990s, that started to change.

It began with "casual Fridays." During the summer, some companies invited their employees to "dress down," or wear more casual clothes to work on Fridays. The policy quickly became popular with employees. After this, it didn't take long for employees to start dressing more casually every day of the week.

Many employees welcomed the new dress policy and the more comfortable work environment that came with it. Etiquette had definitely changed, and suits and ties were rarely seen in many offices. Some employees went as far as wearing jeans, T-shirts, and sneakers to the office. Many people felt that casual attire made the workplace a friendlier place. Co-workers were more relaxed with each other. People enjoyed coming to work knowing it was a comfortable place to be.

Then some people began to change their minds about casual dress at work. Many managers felt that casual dress had led to casual attitudes toward work. Some people started to notice an increase in employees being late to work. If "clothes make the man," as the saying goes, then casual clothes make a casual person who is less committed to company productivity and quality.

One of the biggest reasons why there have been such mixed opinions about dressing down is that there is no real standard for appropriate casual dress. Is it shorts, T-shirts, brightly colored tops, and flip-flops? Is it designer jeans, polo shirts, and trendy sneakers? Is it khakis and sport jackets? Or are Hawaiian shirts and torn jeans OK? Without a casual dress code policy, the etiquette for dress in many companies is beginning to change back to more formal business attire—a style that everyone understands.

casual (adjective):
1. not caring; 2. suitable for everyday use;
3. without attention; 4. not planned

○ ONLINE

INFORMATION SOURCE: www.careerknowhow.com

1. Men used to wear _____ to work in an office.
    a. suits
    b. conservative skirt outfits
    c. jeans and ties

2. Casual Fridays started _____.
    a. about thirty years ago
    b. in the summer
    c. with women

3. Employees in most companies _____ the idea of causal Fridays.
    a. liked
    b. didn't enjoy
    c. didn't know about

4. Now many managers think that employees should _____.
    a. wear jeans
    b. not dress casually
    c. work on casual Friday

5. Etiquette for dressing for work is once again becoming _____ in many companies.
    a. more casual
    b. less professional
    c. more professional

18 WHAT ABOUT YOU? Answer the questions in your <u>own</u> way.

1. How has the etiquette for dressing changed in your country?

_____

2. Is this change for the better?

_____

19 Read about Naomi's problem and give her advice about the etiquette and cultural changes in your country. Use ideas from the box or your own ideas.

"I've been out of the country for over fifteen years. Now I'm back, but so much has changed. I don't know what to do. Can you tell me about the changes in etiquette and culture?"

- clothing customs
- dating customs
- forms of address
- male/female roles in the home
- male/female roles in the workplace
- rules about formal behavior
- rules about punctuality
- table manners

GRAMMAR BOOSTER

A Complete the tag questions. Then look at the picture. Answer each question with a short answer.

1. It's a beautiful day today, _isn't it_ ?   Yes, it is.
2. It's not 2:30 yet, _is it_ ?   No, it isn't.
3. It's a good day to ride a bike, _____ ?   _____
4. The girl on the bike can't see the car, _____ ?   _____
5. Yesterday was Sunday, _____ ?   _____
6. The people haven't met before today, _____ ?   _____
7. They're not cold, _____ ?   _____
8. The man plays tennis, _____ ?   _____

B Complete each sentence with the correct form of the words in parentheses. Use the present continuous or the simple present tense.

1. It ____sounds____ (sound) like they had a great vacation.
2. I _____ (have) English class every Tuesday at 5:30.
3. The children are hungry, so I _____ (make) them sandwiches.
4. Dr. Angle always _____ (tell) her patients to exercise more.
5. Our boss _____ (go) to Cairo next Monday.
6. What _____ you _____ (do) tomorrow evening?
7. The bus _____ (leave) at 3:00 on the weekends.
8. I _____ (bake) a cake for Emma's party tomorrow.

C Complete each sentence in the e-mail with the present perfect or the present perfect continuous.

Dear Sydney,

Hi! How are you? So far, I _____ a great time in Mexico. The sun
                                         1. have
_____ the whole time! I started my trip in Cancún, and spent a
2. shine
few days there. Now I'm in San Cristobál. I _____ here
                                               3. be
before, so it's nice to be back. I _____ some other travelers.
                                        4. meet
They _____ for a long time, so they have a lot of great tips.
       5. travel
We're all going to Oaxaca next. I can't wait!

Talk to you soon!

Chris

D Correct the verbs in the following sentences.

1. Sheila was studying in London when she ~~was meeting~~ met her boyfriend.
2. My family was going to Cairo last summer. It was a great trip!
3. They have know her since 2003.
4. He didn't used to work there, but now he does.
5. I watched a movie when he called, but I didn't mind the interruption.
6. I already seen that movie.
7. We have been traveling to Mexico three times.

WRITING BOOSTER

A Match the emoticon and abbreviation with the phrase that has the same meaning. Write the letter on the line.

1. __b__ ☺
2. ____ LOL
3. ____ IMHO
4. ____ ☹
5. ____ GR8 2 C U
6. ____ BTW
7. ____ LMK
8. ____ C U L8R
9. ____ R U OK?

a. "Let me know."
b. "I'm smiling."
c. "I'm not happy."
d. "Laughing out loud"
e. "By the way"
f. "In my humble opinion"
g. "See you later."
h. "Great to see you."
i. "Are you okay?"

B Complete the chart. Write the letter of the things you should do and the things you shouldn't do in formal e-mail etiquette.

a. Use a title, last name, and colon to address someone you don't know well.
b. Write in complete sentences.
c. Use correct spelling.
d. Use emoticons.
e. Use all lower-case letters.
f. Punctuate carefully.
g. Date the e-mail.
h. End with your name.
i. Close the e-mail as a formal letter, for example, *Thank you so much*.
j. Include abbreviations.
k. Use a first name and comma to address someone you know well.

Do's: __a_____
Don'ts: __d_____

C Read the following e-mail and circle all the formal e-mail etiquette errors. Then, on a separate sheet of paper, rewrite the e-mail and correct the etiquette errors.

Maria, Thanks 4 lunch yesterday. it was GR8 2 C U. let's continue our conversation about the project. maybe Wednesday next week? My place? There's still lots 2 discus. ☹ BTW, please don't forget to bring the info we talked about.
LMK about next week. C U L8R.
Peter

UNIT 2 Health Matters

Preview

1 What dental emergency does each person have? Write <u>broken tooth</u>, <u>lost filling</u>, <u>loose tooth</u>, <u>swollen gums</u>, or <u>toothache</u> on the line. You will not use all of the phrases

"I have a terrible pain in my tooth. I need to find a dentist as soon as possible."

1. _____

"They've been bothering me since yesterday. They're all red and painful."

2. _____

"I'm in a lot of pain. I hear you can put chewing gum in the hole until you see the dentist."

3. _____

"A piece of it broke off when I was eating candy yesterday. Luckily, it doesn't hurt that much."

4. _____

2 **WHAT ABOUT YOU?** Which of the following health-related items do you take when you travel?

☐ extra medication
☐ an extra pair of glasses or contact lenses
☐ special food
☐ exercise clothes or equipment
☐ the name and number of a doctor at your destination
☐ other: _____

Here are a few tips to maintain good dental health:

- You should brush your teeth at least twice a day, especially after meals.
- Brush your teeth for at least two minutes each time you brush.
  (Try timing yourself. Very few people actually brush for this long.)
- Brush gently with a soft toothbrush. Brushing too hard can hurt your teeth and gums.
- Don't forget to brush your tongue and the roof of your mouth.
- Change your toothbrush every three to four months.

3 Complete the conversations. Choose the letter of the correct answer.

1. A: I hear you're from England.
   B: _____
   a. London.
   b. Yes, I am.
   c. I really appreciate it.

2. A: Thanks for fitting me in.
   B: _____
   a. Would you like me to make an appointment for you?
   b. If you could. Thanks.
   c. Luckily, I had a cancellation.

3. A: _____
   B: Well, let's have a look.
   a. Can you recommend a dentist?
   b. Actually, there's one not far from here.
   c. This tooth is killing me.

4. A: I need to see a dentist. I think it's an emergency.
   B: _____
   a. Thanks for fitting me in.
   b. OK, there's one not far from here.
   c. When did it first begin to hurt?

LESSON 1

4 Write the word from the box that matches each definition. You will not use all the words.

| chest | coughing | dizzy | hip | nauseous |
| short of breath | sneezing | stomach | weak | wheezing |

1. _____ part of the body between the neck and stomach
2. _____ not strong, without energy
3. _____ feeling that you're going to vomit
4. _____ making a noise by air suddenly coming out of the nose
5. _____ suddenly pushing air out of the throat with a short sound
6. _____ part of the body below the chest and above the legs

5 Complete the statements with <u>must</u> or <u>must not</u> to draw conclusions.

1. He hasn't slept for two days. He _____ tired.
                                        be
2. If Heather didn't eat any pizza, she _____ well. She loves pizza.
                                              feel
3. Tim broke his leg. It _____ a lot.
                              hurt
4. She's been sneezing all day. She _____ a cold.
                                          have
5. Karen hasn't left yet. She _____ in a hurry.
                                    be
6. Bob's allergies are bothering him today. He _____ to go hiking with us.
                                                      want

6 Look at the pictures. Complete each sentence with <u>must</u> or <u>must not</u> to draw conclusions.

1. He _____ be getting a checkup.
2. He _____ be going on vacation.
3. She _____ like the dark.
4. The dog _____ want to go swimming.
5. She _____ have gloves with her.
6. She _____ be feeling well.

7 WHAT ABOUT YOU? Think about the last time you were sick. Fill in this patient information form from a doctor's office.

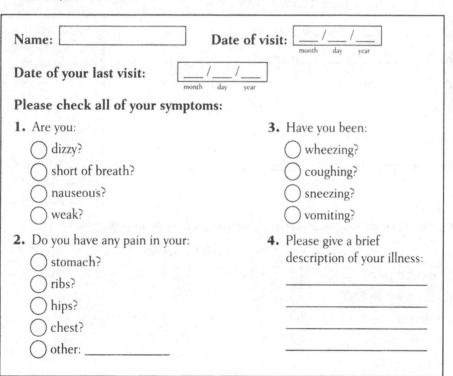

"An apple a day keeps the doctor away."

—This line comes from an old poem that was told to children to encourage them to eat healthy foods like fruits and vegetables. It's still a common saying today in English.

Health Matters 91

LESSON 2

8 Complete each sentence with a word from the box.

| a blood test | a checkup | an EKG | a shot | an X-ray |

1. The nurse will take a sample of blood so _____ can be done.
2. The doctor will give you the medicine by giving you _____ in the arm.
3. The doctor is going to take _____ to look at the broken bone.
4. _____ records electrical signals from the heart's activity.
5. I'm going to the doctor for _____ to make sure that I'm healthy.

9 Complete the conversation. Use the words and phrases from the box. You will not use all of the words and phrases.

| an appointment | appreciate | chest | a checkup | an EKG |
| fit | an injection | need | a pain | a toothache |

Receptionist: Hello, Dr. Winters' office.

Alexander York: Hello. I'm calling because I'd like to make _____ to see the doctor.
1.
I have _____ in my _____.
  2.   3.

Receptionist: I think you might need _____. Let's see—
  4.
I can _____ you in this afternoon.
  5.
Would you be able to come in at 4:00?

Alexander York: Yes, that's great. I really _____ it.
  6.

Pictures taken with X-rays show inside the body because different parts of it absorb the rays of radiation at different rates. Calcium in bones absorbs the most radiation, so bones look white on an X-ray image (also called a radiograph). Fat and other softer body parts absorb less and look gray. Air absorbs the least amount of radiation, so lungs look black on an X-ray.

INFORMATION SOURCE: http://science.howstuffworks.com

10 Now answer these questions about the conversation. Check yes, no, or no information.

	yes	no	no information
1. Does Mr. York have chest pain?	☐	☐	☐
2. Does the receptionist need an EKG?	☐	☐	☐
3. Is Mr. York from overseas?	☐	☐	☐
4. Can the doctor see Mr. York today?	☐	☐	☐
5. Does Mr. York need a checkup?	☐	☐	☐

11 Circle the word that correctly completes each sentence.

1. The dentist **may** / **will** be able to see you today, but I'm not sure.
2. Your gums are really swollen. You **might** / **must** be in a lot of pain.
3. Bill hates to miss class. He **must** / **might** be really sick if he's not here today.
4. We **will** / **might** be able to go shopping this weekend. It depends on if we have time.
5. You lost a filling? That **must** / **may** really hurt!
6. The patient **might** / **must** need a blood test. The doctor will have to examine him to be sure.
7. Susan **will** / **must** be able to meet us for dinner, but she said she'd be a little late.

12 Rewrite each sentence using <u>may</u>, <u>might</u>, or <u>must</u> and <u>be able to</u>.

1. She has a lot of work to do, so she _might not be able to_ keep her doctor's appointment.
2. Dr. Morris isn't in until this afternoon. He _____ see you.
3. I'm sorry, but I have to cancel today. I _____ see you until the end of the week. I'll have to check my schedule.
4. If I leave work at 5:00, I _____ get there by 5:30. It depends on how much traffic there is.
5. Mrs. Graham has called several dentists. She _____ get an appointment for today.

LESSON 3

13 Read the article *Consider the Choices* on page 20 in the Student's Book again. Write the names of the treatments.

1. When modern medicine and surgeries are unsuccessful, a person might try one of these treatments.
   _____

2. A person who is afraid of needles would not want this treatment.
   _____

3. A person who needs surgery would want this treatment.
   _____

4. A person who feels strongly that there is a mind and body connection would choose this treatment.
   _____

5. A lot of conventional medicines are based on the study of this treatment.
   _____

6. A person who is using a remedy that can actually cause the symptoms the person suffers from is using this treatment.
   _____

14 WHAT ABOUT YOU? What are some pros and cons of each type of treatment? Use your <u>own</u> ideas.

	Pros	Cons
acupuncture	It can help you quit smoking. It's 5,000 years old, so it must work.	I don't like needles!
conventional medicine		
herbal therapy		
homeopathy		
spiritual healing		

15 Read the website about a type of medical treatment. Then circle the letter of the answer that correctly completes each sentence.

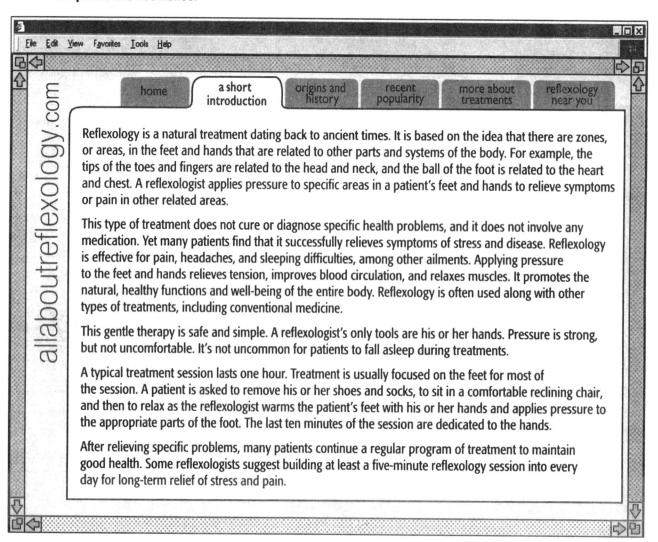

INFORMATION SOURCE: www.reflexology.org

1. A reflexologist is a _____.
   a. person who provides reflexology treatment
   b. patient
   c. person who receives reflexology treatment
   d. doctor

2. The article doesn't mention that reflexology can relieve _____.
   a. headaches
   b. problems with the feet
   c. tension
   d. symptoms of disease

3. Reflexology _____ with other treatments.
   a. can be combined
   b. is never combined
   c. isn't usually combined
   d. might be combined in the future

4. In a typical session of reflexology, about _____ is spent on the feet.
   a. one hour
   b. fifty minutes
   c. ten minutes
   c. half the time

5. The ideas behind reflexology are most similar to those of _____.
   a. conventional medicine
   b. spiritual healing
   c. herbal therapy
   d. acupuncture

16 Complete the chart. Use the information from the website in Exercise 14 and the Reading on page 20 in the Student's Book.

Type of treatment	How it's similar to reflexology	How it's different from reflexology
homeopathy		
herbal therapy		
acupuncture		

LESSON 4

17 Suggest medications for the following symptoms. In some cases, more than one type might be helpful. Explain why you think each medication is helpful.

Symptom	Medication	Reason
sneezing	Cold tablets,	
a toothache		
weakness		
coughing		
stomach problems		
a burn from hot oil		
red eyes		
an infection		

Health Matters   95

18 WHAT ABOUT YOU? How do you buy medications in your country? Which ones do you need a prescription for? Which ones can you buy without a prescription? Which are available both ways?

	Prescription always needed	Prescription not needed	Some kinds require a prescription
antacids	☐	☐	☐
painkillers	☐	☐	☐
antibiotics	☐	☐	☐
vitamins	☐	☐	☐
cold tablets	☐	☐	☐
antihistamines	☐	☐	☐
other: _____	☐	☐	☐

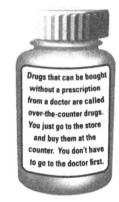

Drugs that can be bought without a prescription from a doctor are called over-the-counter drugs. You just go to the store and buy them at the counter. You don't have to go to the doctor first.

19 WHAT ABOUT YOU? Answer the questions in your <u>own</u> way.

1. What are some of the medications listed in Exercise 18 that you have taken? _____
_____

2. What is the normal dosage? _____

3. Do you need a prescription to get them? _____

4. What are some warnings or side effects of these medicines? _____
_____

GRAMMAR BOOSTER

A Rewrite the sentences, using <u>probably</u> and <u>most likely</u>.

1. He feels terrible. He must have the flu.
_____

2. My arm aches. It must be from the shot I got yesterday.
_____

3. My doctor is not answering the phone. He must not be in today.
_____

4. An herbalist must know a lot of different plants.
_____

5. Lucy is not eating anything. She must not be feeling well.
_____

B **Rewrite each sentence with <u>maybe</u>.**

1. She's been sneezing since she got here. She may be allergic to my cat.
   _____

2. I'm not feeling well. I may have the flu.
   _____

3. He's taking a lot of medication. He may be sick.
   _____

4. He has pain in his chest. He may need an EKG.
   _____

5. She hates to fly. She may prefer to take the train.
   _____

6. It looks like a bad infection. The doctor may want to prescribe antibiotics.
   _____

C **Each sentence below has an error. Rewrite each sentence correctly.**

1. I think I forgot probably to take my medication.
   _____

2. He doesn't have a fever. May be it's just a cold.
   _____

3. She is dizzy because she doesn't most likely get enough sleep.
   _____

4. We don't have probably any cough medicine at home.
   _____

5. He maybe able to return to work tomorrow.
   _____

6. He likes natural medicine so he prefers probably herbal therapy.
   _____

7. They're late probably because they overslept.
   _____

8. She prefers maybe to wait until Monday.
   _____

WRITING BOOSTER

A Read the sentences. Are they comparing or contrasting things? Check the correct answer.

	Comparison	Contrast
1. My sister is different from my brother in the way she acts toward her friends.		
2. Vegetables are healthy and low in carbohydrates. Likewise, fruit is healthy even though it is higher in carbohydrates.		
3. Unlike New York, San Diego is on the west coast.		
4. High school and college are alike in many ways.		
5. Riding a bicycle is good exercise. On the other hand, driving a car uses little energy.		
6. If you have an infection, you can take antibiotics, but if you have the flu, the antibiotics will not work.		
7. Many of the subjects he is studying require a lot of reading. They also require essay writing.		
8. A broken ankle is very painful. A sprained ankle is very painful as well.		
9. I enjoy traveling by train. However, I really dislike plane travel.		
10. Both Saturday and Sunday are my favorite days of the week.		

B Circle the word that correctly completes each sentence.

1. A very painful ankle may require an X-ray. A painful tooth may require one, _____.
   a. too
   b. similarly

2. _____ acupuncture and spiritual healing are considered holistic medicine, not conventional medicine.
   a. Whereas
   b. Both

3. Doctors that prescribe conventional medications must have a medical degree. _____, doctors that prescribe natural medications don't have to have one.
   a. On the other hand
   b. Likewise

4. _____ a slight headache, a severe headache might need a painkiller.
   a. Whereas
   b. Unlike

5. You need a prescription to buy antibiotics. _____, you don't need a prescription to buy vitamins or some painkillers.
   a. However
   b. Similarly

C Look at the chart comparing Chinese health massage and acupuncture. On a separate sheet of paper, write a short paragraph comparing the two. Use these ideas or your own ideas.

Chinese health massage	Acupuncture
has been used for a very long time	has been used for thousands of years
increases energy flow in the body	increases energy flow throughout the body
helps the body's immune or defense system	improves the body's immune or defense system

D Look at the chart contrasting the Japanese and American healthcare systems. On a separate sheet of paper, write a short paragraph contrasting the two. Use these ideas or your own ideas.

Japanese healthcare system	American healthcare system
universal healthcare system (available to all citizens)	not universal
Japanese employees pay more for healthcare if they are overweight.	American employees do not pay more if they are overweight.
Healthcare companies are not allowed to make a profit.	Healthcare companies can make a profit.
Employers are encouraged to check the weight of employees. Higher weight tends to indicate a less healthy employee.	Employers cannot check the weight of employees. It is against the law.

INFORMATION SOURCE: www.bukisa.com/articles/216630

UNIT 3 Getting Things Done

Preview

1 Look at the pictures. Which person is a procrastinator? Which person is well-organized? Check (✓) the correct box.

"Oh, no! I have to get these pressed for my interview today!"

"I need to get this package to Jakarta by Wednesday. Do you think it will get there in two days?"

"I'd like 100 more pages just like this by next week, OK?"

1. ☐ procrastinator ☐ well-organized
2. ☐ procrastinator ☐ well-organized
3. ☐ procrastinator ☐ well-organized

"I need 50 copies of my report printed from this CD for my meeting in Beijing next month."

"What a mess! And the guests are coming in an hour!"

4. ☐ procrastinator ☐ well-organized
5. ☐ procrastinator ☐ well-organized

> "Procrastination is the art of keeping up with yesterday and avoiding today."
>
> ~Wayne Dyer

2 Match the sentences with similar meanings. Draw a line.

1. I have a really urgent job.
2. I've got a lot on my plate.
3. I need this a.s.a.p.
4. I won't keep you then.
5. I owe you one.
6. No sweat.

a. I am really busy.
b. I have to get this done as soon as possible.
c. I don't want to take up more of your time.
d. I'm working on a really important task.
e. No problem.
f. I really appreciate your help.

LESSON 1

3 Circle the word or phrase that best completes each sentence.

1. You can have someone **do / does / to do** that for you.
2. The lawyer will make them **signed / sign / to sign** the papers.
3. She got a service **to clean / cleaned / clean** her house before the party.
4. Why don't you get someone **helped / to help / help** you?
5. Mrs. Oliver always makes people **to do / did / do** whatever she wants.
6. Have someone else **taken / to take / take** care of that.

4 Complete the paragraph with the correct form of the verbs.

BEFORE:

My life used to be so crazy. I tried to do everything myself, and I never got anyone _____ me. Then I realized that it's OK to have other people _____ a few things
1. help   2. do
for me. For example, now I make the kids _____ their rooms themselves. And I have my
3. clean
husband _____ at the grocery store on his way home from work if I need something.
4. stop
I've even gotten the kids _____ a little bit. It's not always the best food, but at least I
5. cook
don't have to do it! I've found that my life is much calmer when I have everyone _____
6. share
the responsibilities.

AFTER:

5 Match each request with a similar sentence. Write the letter on the line.

_____ 1. Would you fill in for me at the soccer game this weekend?   a. Can you get it?

_____ 2. Is it possible for you to give me a ride home?   b. Can I use it?

_____ 3. Will you pick up dinner on your way home?   c. Could you watch it?

_____ 4. Could you lend me your phone for a minute?   d. Can you drive me?

_____ 5. Would you keep an eye on the soup?   e. Could you take my place?

6
Complete the conversation. Use the words in the box. You will not use all of the words.

get	favor	fill in for	have	lend
lifesaver	owe	pick up	problem	understand

Anna: Hey, Greg. Are you busy? Could you do me a _____1._____?

Greg: No _____2._____. What can I do for you?

Anna: Well, I have a meeting in a few minutes, but I need to _____3._____ some documents from the copy place down the street.

Greg: Why don't you _____4._____ them deliver the documents?

Anna: I'm afraid that might be difficult. There's no time.

Greg: I _____5._____.

Anna: Thanks a million, Greg. You're a _____6._____.

Greg: No sweat. You just _____7._____ me one.

LESSON 2

7
What kind of service does each person want to have done? Use the words in the box.

copying	printing	haircut	delivery
dry cleaning	framing	shoe repair	

"I just bought this great poster. Now I need to get it fixed so that I can hang it above my desk."

1. _framing_

"Can you shorten it by about 3 inches?"

2. _____

"Could I have these packages in my office by noon?"

3. _____

"I need this sweater done a.s.a.p. It's urgent."

4. _____

"I lost the heel on these sandals. Can you fix it for me?"

5. _____

"Can you have this sign for me by tomorrow?"

6. _____

"I have to get more handouts for tomorrow's meeting."

7. _____

8 Read the services in Exercise 7. Complete the sentences with the service each person needs. Use the passive causative.

1. He would like to have _his poster framed_.
2. She wants to get _____.
3. He would like to have _____.
4. She needs to have _____.
5. She wants to have _____.
6. He needs to get _____.
7. He has to get _____.

9 Complete each sentence with the passive causative. Use the correct tense.

1. We _will have the sign copied_ tomorrow because the printer is closed today.

have / the sign / copy
2. Don't _____ there. They've lost my shirts twice!

have / your shirts / press
3. Can you please _____ before this afternoon's meeting?

get / these pages / copy
4. Last week I _____, and now it looks like new.

have / my blouse / dry-clean
5. Mr. Sutton needs to _____ today.

have / these flowers / deliver
6. Would it be possible to _____ by this afternoon?

get / this photo / print
7. Bill's pants were too long, but then yesterday, he _____.

have / them / shorten
8. Sometime next week she _____.

get / her computer / repair

10 CHALLENGE. Correct the mistake in each sentence.

1. You can have the packages ~~delivering~~ _delivered_ to your home or office.
2. If you're getting (dry-cleaned) your suit, make sure you can pick it up tomorrow.
3. You can have your shoes repair for much less than it costs to buy a new pair.
4. We're having signs to print to announce the big event next week.
5. Where did you got your pants lengthened? They did a great job.
6. You should get your skirt shorten so it looks more fashionable.
7. I'd like to have framed this diploma so I can hang it up.
8. They didn't had the house cleaned yesterday.

11 WHAT ABOUT YOU? Which services do you use? Complete each sentence in your own way. Use the passive causative.

1. I always have _____.
2. I've never had _____.
3. I have gotten _____.
4. Sometimes I get _____.

LESSON 3

12 Read the article *The Tailors of Hong Kong* on page 32 in the Student's Book again. Check <u>true</u>, <u>false</u>, or <u>no information</u>.

	true	false	no information
1. You used to be able to have a suit tailored in 24 hours in Hong Kong.	☐	☐	☐
2. There are still a lot of places in Hong Kong that can make a garment in just one day.	☐	☐	☐
3. If you buy a ready-made garment at a store at home, it will cost about the same as a custom-made garment in Hong Kong.	☐	☐	☐
4. If the garment doesn't fit, you will need to pay more money to have it fixed.	☐	☐	☐
5. A deposit is required before the tailor starts working on your garment.	☐	☐	☐
6. If you don't like the garment you ordered, you can get all your money back.	☐	☐	☐

13 Read the article. Then write <u>T</u> for <u>true</u> or <u>F</u> for <u>false</u> for each statement, according to the information in the article. Correct the false statements.

"Dry" cleaning

When you need your delicate garments cleaned, you take them to your local dry cleaning store. You give them your clothes, get a ticket, and after a few hours or a few days, your clothes are as good as new. But do you know what dry cleaning is? Do you know how it first started?

Despite its name, dry cleaning is actually not a dry process. Clothes are washed in liquid chemicals, but without water. (That's why the process became known as *dry cleaning*.) Dry cleaning is often used instead of washing delicate fabrics by hand. It can also remove stains that can't be removed at home.

The invention of dry cleaning was an accident. In 1855, a Frenchman named Jean Baptiste Jolly made a discovery: A lamp filled with kerosene fell on a greasy cloth in his home (kerosene is a type of oil that burns well). When the kerosene dried, the cloth was cleaner where the liquid had been.

Based on this discovery, people began to use chemicals to clean clothes. But most of these chemicals, such as kerosene and gasoline, could easily catch on fire, so dry cleaning was very dangerous.

In the 1930s, people started to use a new chemical, called *percholoroethylene*, or *perc* for short. This chemical cleaned well, was gentle on most fabrics, and most importantly, it didn't catch on fire easily, so it was much safer than the chemicals that were used earlier. It is still used today by most dry cleaners. However, in recent years, some people have been worried about possible health issues related to perc.

While perc does not catch on fire easily, people who work in dry cleaning shops have complained of dizziness, headaches, sleepiness, sore eyes and throat, and other more serious illnesses from the chemical smells. Some new machines have been developed to help keep the fumes from escaping during the cleaning process and to keep the air in the shops cleaner, fresher, and safer.

INFORMATION SOURCE: science.howstuffworks.com

_____ 1. No liquid is used in the dry cleaning process.

_____ 2. Jean Baptiste Jolly was trying to find a new way to clean clothes.

_____ 3. When kerosene got on the cloth in Jolly's home, the cloth caught on fire.

_____ 4. Kerosene can clean greasy cloth.

_____ 5. People stopped using gasoline and kerosene because they were dangerous.

_____ 6. Perc doesn't burn as easily as kerosene and gasoline.

_____ 7. Perc isn't used in dry cleaning anymore.

14 Read the article again. Then answer the questions.

1. How is dry cleaning different from the way people normally wash their clothes at home?
   _____

2. What chemicals did people use to dry-clean their clothes in the late 1800s?
   _____

3. Why did people start using perc for dry cleaning?
   _____

15 Look at the completed customer survey. Then answer the questions about the customer's experience. Write **yes**, **no**, or **no information**.

> Thank you for choosing **Sew Clean** for your tailoring and dry cleaning needs. We want to know about your experience. Please take a moment to complete this survey and evaluate our quality of service.
>
> | | 5 excellent | 4 good | 3 average | 2 poor | 1 unacceptable |
> |---|---|---|---|---|---|
> | Quality of work | ⑤ | 4 | 3 | 2 | 1 |
> | Speed of service | 5 | ④ | 3 | 2 | 1 |
> | Price of service | 5 | 4 | 3 | ② | 1 |
> | Knowledge of employees | ⑤ | 4 | 3 | 2 | 1 |
>
> Do you have any other comments? The tailor knew what she was doing. She shortened my pants perfectly. And they were ready on time. She told me that they would be finished the next day, and they were!

1. Does the customer think that the business is efficient? _____
2. Does the customer think that the business is professional? _____
3. Does the customer think that the prices are reasonable? _____
4. Does the customer think that the employees are helpful? _____
5. Does the customer think that the employees are reliable? _____
6. Does the customer think that the business offers a lot of different services? _____
7. Did the customer use the tailoring services? _____
8. Did the customer use the dry cleaning services? _____

16 Read and respond to the instant message. Describe the quality of the service and the workmanship of one business in your area.

```
Rudy425
File  Edit  Actions  Tools  Help

rudy425: I'm new to the area and would really like to know about the local services. Can you recommend any businesses?
you: _____
_____
_____
_____
_____
```

LESSON 4

17 Look at the plans for the party. Answer the questions.

Plans for Shannon's surprise party:

- **Mike:** call Shannon's family to see who to invite
  write down all the friends who we'll invite

- **Kayla:** call friends and family to see when they are available
  decide which day most people can come

- **Alan:** visit Bryce Park and Shady Grove
  decide which one is best for the party

- **Ryan:** decide how to spend the money

- **Page:** let everyone know about the party

- **Abby:** buy balloons and "Happy Birthday" sign
  get place ready for party

- **Samantha:** get information and compare prices of food

- **Carrie:** find someone to provide music

1. Who is going to pick a date? _____
2. Who is going to arrange catering? _____
3. Who is going to make a list of attendees? _____
4. Who is going to pick a place? _____
5. Who is going to arrange music? _____
6. Who is going to set up the place? _____
7. Who is going to send out invitations? _____
8. Who is going to make a budget? _____

18 WHAT ABOUT YOU? Answer the questions in your own way.

1. Which step for planning a social event would you most like to do? Why?
_____
_____

2. Which step would you least like to do? Why?
_____
_____

19 Read the article. Then circle the letter of the correct answer to each question.

HOW TO ENJOY YOUR OWN PARTY

Sometimes hosts are so busy planning a party that they don't enjoy themselves at the actual event. Here are some tips to help you relax and have fun!

Make lists of:
- everything you're going to clean
- how you'll decorate
- food that you'll serve
- stores you need to go to (grocery store, florist, party store, etc.)
- personal preparations (buy an outfit, get hair done, shower, etc.)

- Assign cleaning, cooking, decorating, and other responsibilities. Have your family and friends help, or hire someone.
- Decide which foods you can make before the day of the party. Have a caterer make everything else.
- Make a schedule for the day of the party. Include cleaning and decorating tasks as well as personal preparations.

Now, follow the schedule you've made, and enjoy the party!

1. According to the article, you'll enjoy your own party more if you _____.
   a. plan for it well
   b. look fabulous
   c. serve delicious food

2. Make lists to help you _____.
   a. choose which foods to serve
   b. make a hair appointment
   c. plan

3. You should make food _____ the party.
   a. during
   b. before the day of
   c. on the day of

4. The article doesn't mention _____.
   a. getting people to help you
   b. shopping
   c. how to choose the menu

20 WHAT ABOUT YOU? Answer the questions in your own way.

1. What do you think is most important at a party? Rate the details from 1 to 5, 1 being the most important, 5 being the least important.

    ____ music

    ____ food

    ____ decorations

    ____ place

    ____ other: _____

2. Explain why you think that _____ is the most important detail in party planning.

    _____
    _____

3. What are some reasons for having a party?

    _____   _____   _____
    _____   _____   _____

GRAMMAR BOOSTER

A
Look at the chart about what each child is permitted to do. Complete each item with information from the chart. Use let.

	Go to bed late	Eat a lot of sugar	Stay home from school
Tina	✗	✓	✓
John	✓	✗	✗
Michael and Jim	✓	✓	✗

1. Tina's parents _don't let her go_ to bed late. But they _let her eat_ a lot of sugar. And sometimes they _____ home from school.

2. John's mother _____ to bed late. But she _____ a lot of sugar. And she _____ home from school either.

3. Michael and Jim's parents _____ to bed late. They also _____ a lot of sugar. But they _____ home from school.

B
Read each statement. Give advice about what the person should or shouldn't permit. Use let or don't let.

1. "The kids are running all over the house."

    YOU: _Let them play outside._ OR _Don't let them climb on the furniture._

2. "My daughter broke a tooth on a piece of candy."

    YOU: _____

3. "My little sister watches too much TV"

    YOU: _____

C **Read each sentence and then answer the question.**

1. We had made some cookies for the kids. Who made the cookies? _We did._
2. Lisa had her parents send in the form. Who sent in the form? _____
3. They had their friends move the furniture. Who moved the furniture? _____
4. Jeff's boss, Brian, had cancelled the meeting. Who cancelled the meeting? _____
5. We had talked to the clients about the problem. Who talked about the problem? _____
6. Taylor had Steve take the messages for Christine. Who took the messages? _____

D **Read each sentence. Cross out the <u>by</u> phrase if it is not important.**

1. I had my shirt's sleeves shortened ~~by someone~~.
2. The gallery always gets things framed by Colin's Frames.
3. We get our holiday cookies made by a professional bakery down the street.
4. You should get your photos printed by the people at the mall.
5. They're having the package sent by Zipp's Delivery Service.
6. She got the kids' pictures taken by the person with the camera.
7. I get my clothes dry-cleaned by a person at Summit Cleaners.
8. She always gets her hair cut by Clara at Shear Perfection.

WRITING BOOSTER

A **Write a sentence expressing your personal opinion in response to each of the following questions. Use expressions for stating opinions from the chart on page 142 in the Student's Book.**

1. Do you think people who are very organized get more done with less stress?
   _____
2. Do you think it's important for people to get along at work?
   _____
3. Do you think children should be required to study music at school?
   _____
4. Do you think getting people to help is better than trying to do everything yourself?
   _____
5. Do you think speed and reliability are the most important reasons to choose one store over another?
   _____
6. Do you think employers should be allowed to check their employees' health?
   _____

B Complete each statement with a personal example.

1. I'm a very organized person. For example, _____
   _____.

2. Some people are good at making a budget, but I am not one of them. Whenever _____
   _____
   _____.

3. I feel great every time _____
   _____.

4. There are a lot of times I have to run late for an appointment. For instance, _____
   _____.

5. I used to be a terrible procrastinator. When I was _____
   _____.

6. The people where I live are so nice, and they always help me in a lot ways, such as ____
   _____
   _____.

C Look at the opinions you stated in Exercise A. Choose one opinion and list three personal examples to support your view. Use the expressions for stating personal examples from Exercise C.

Your opinion: _____

Personal examples:

1 _____
_____
_____

2 _____
_____
_____

3 _____
_____
_____

UNIT 4
Reading for Pleasure

Preview

 1 Read the book covers. Write the type of book. Use the types from the box. You will not use all of the types.

| an autobiography | a biography | a mystery | a romance novel |
| science fiction | a self-help book | short stories | a travel book |

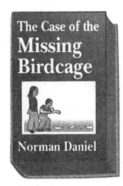

1. _____   2. _____   3. _____

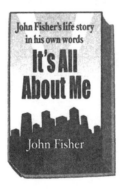

4. _____   5. _____   6. _____

 2 Read each pair of sentences. Write "=" if the sentences have the same or similar meanings and "≠" if the sentences have different meanings.

1. I can't get into it.   ≠   I can't put it down.
2. It's not my thing.   ____   I don't like it.
3. I can't put it down.   ____   It's a real page-turner.
4. I can't get into it.   ____   I can't get enough of it.
5. It puts me to sleep.   ____   I really like it.
6. I'll lend it to you.   ____   You can borrow it.
7. I'm just browsing.   ____   I'm looking for a specific book.

> " A room without books is like a body without a soul. "
> — **Marcus Tullius Cicero** (Ancient Roman politician, writer, and public speaker)
>
> **Source:** www.seasonedwithlove.com

111

3 WHAT ABOUT YOU? Answer the questions in your own way.

1. Name a book or other reading material that you can't get enough of.
   _____

2. Name a book or other reading material that puts you to sleep.
   _____

LESSON 1

4 Read each sentence. Check true or false.

	true	false
1. A page-turner describes a book that you can't put down.	☐	☐
2. If you think a book is a cliff-hanger, you probably can't get into it.	☐	☐
3. A book becomes a best-seller when a lot of people buy it.	☐	☐
4. A book that is a fast read is very difficult.	☐	☐
5. A book that is trash isn't usually considered to be good literature.	☐	☐

5 Respond to each question with a clause using that. Use the prompts.

1. What's in the latest issue of *Car Magazine*? (an article on hybrid cars / I think)
   I think that the latest issue of Car Magazine has an article on hybrid cars.

2. What do you think about this book? (hard to follow / I believe)
   _____

3. What book did she write? (a book about English grammar / I think)
   _____

4. Where do Stieg Larsson's novels take place? (in Sweden / I guess)
   _____

5. Who are the main characters in the *Twilight* novel? (Bella and Edward / I believe)
   _____

6. What is Adam Johnson's short story "Hurricanes Anonymous" about? (a single father / I think)
   _____

7. What is Alice Sebold's most famous novel? (*The Lovely Bones* / I suppose)
   _____

8. They don't have any articles on knitting in this magazine, do they? (disappointed / I)
   _____

6 **WHAT ABOUT YOU?** Complete the sentences in your own way. Use noun clauses.

1. I believe (that) _____.
2. I used to think (that) _____.
3. I didn't know (that) _____.
4. I'm sure (that) _____.
5. I'm happy (that) _____.

7 Write the letter of the sentence that best answers each question.

____ 1. Has Kristin Hannah stopped writing novels?
____ 2. Are you reading anything good these days?
____ 3. Do you think the new Jody Picoult novel is going to be any good?
____ 4. Is your book any good?
____ 5. Have you read anything by Amy Tan?

a. I think so, but I can't remember the title.
b. I hope not. I really like her books.
c. I'm afraid not. I'm surprised I can't find anything good.
d. I believe so. I've just started reading it.
e. I guess so. All of her books are great.

8 Complete each conversation with a logical response. Use so or not.

1. **A:** Does this magazine cost less than this book?
   B: I think ____.
2. **A:** I'm glad the interview went well. Do you think they'll offer you a job?
   B: I hope ____. I really like the company.
3. **A:** Is Scott going to meet us tonight?
   B: Well, he's already an hour late, so I guess ____.
4. **A:** Is it going to rain for our picnic tomorrow?
   B: I hope ____.
5. **A:** Do the stores close at 4:00 in the afternoon?
   B: I don't believe ____.

9 **WHAT ABOUT YOU?** Complete the conversation in your own way. Recommend a book to a friend. Explain why you recommend it.

Your friend: I'm looking for something good to read. Do you have any recommendations?

YOU You should read _____. I highly recommend it.

Your friend: Really? Why's that?

YOU _____
_____
_____

Reading for Pleasure 113

LESSON 2

10 Put the conversation in order. Write the number on the line.

_____ I know. I think I bought the last copy.
_____ Yes, I just bought it at the newsstand downstairs.
_____ I'll lend it to you when I'm done with it.
_____ I was just down there, but it's sold out.
_____ Really? That's great. Thanks.
_____ Is this the latest issue?
_____ Too bad. There's an article in there I really want to read.

> "Tell me what you read and I shall tell you what you are."
> — anonymous proverb

INFORMATION SOURCE: www.seasonedwithlove.com

11 Look at the pictures and complete each sentence. Make embedded questions.

1. She would like to know _if (whether) Red Thunder is the author's second novel_.

2. He'd like to know _____.

3. She wonders _____.

4. He wonders _____.

12 Read each pair of embedded questions. Circle the letter of the correct sentence in each pair.

1. a. I don't know if it's trash.
   b. I don't know if is it trash.

2. a. Would you mind asking Angie whether I could see her book?
   b. Would you mind asking Angie that I could see her book?

114   UNIT 4

3. a. Do you know why Helen Keller wrote about her life?
   b. Do you know why did Helen Keller write about her life?
4. a. I wonder who is Anne's new friend.
   b. I wonder who Anne's new friend is.
5. a. Tell me when did you get this.
   b. Tell me when you got this.
6. a. Could you tell me where the children's books are?
   b. Could you tell me where are the children's books?

13 Circle the word that correctly completes each embedded question.
1. I wonder **whether** / **who** John Steinbeck wrote this.
2. I'd like to know **if** / **that** anyone recommends reading this book.
3. Do you know **who** / **when** you bought it?
4. Tell me **what** / **whether** this book is about.
5. I don't know **what** / **if** the book is available online or not.

14 Change each sentence to an embedded question. Begin each question in a different way.
1. Who took my novel? _I'd like to know who took my novel. OR Tell me who took my novel._ _OR I wonder who took my novel._
2. Is this a best-seller?
3. Why didn't you finish reading this?
4. When did she write her memoir?
5. Who is this present for?
6. Do you like to read non-fiction?
7. Are we ready to go to the library?

15 WHAT ABOUT YOU? Complete the sentences with embedded questions in your own way.
1. I don't know _____.
2. I wonder _____.
3. I'd like to know _____.

Reading for Pleasure 115

LESSON 3

16 Complete the paragraphs with the phrases in the box.

| curled up with | did puzzles | listened to an audio book |
| read aloud | read the travel section online | skimmed through |

Yesterday, Madison Jeffries and her mom started the day by looking at the paper. They didn't have plans for the weekend, so they quickly _____1._____ the entertainment section of the newspaper to see what events were going on around town. Then they _____2._____ because their family is planning a vacation and they're not sure where to go. So they looked at several articles about places that they thought were interesting.

Later that day, Madison went with her mom for a car ride. Since it was a long trip and they didn't want to get bored, they _____3._____ in the car. When they got home, they _____4._____ together. Her mom helped her figure out the items she couldn't answer.

At the end of the day, Madison got ready for bed, and her mother _____5._____ to her. After Madison fell asleep, her mother _____6._____ a romance novel.

17 Look at the pictures and label them with the phrases from the box in Exercise 16. Then number the activities in the order they occurred in the paragraph.

a. _____ ☐   b. _____ ☐   c. _____ ☐

d. _____ ☐   e. _____ ☐   f. _____ ☐

116 UNIT 4

18 WHAT ABOUT YOU? Answer the questions with your own information.

1. What time of day do you usually read? _____
2. Do you mostly read for pleasure or for school / work? _____
3. Where do you like to read? _____
4. Do you like to hear other noise (music, television, etc.) when you read? Why or why not?
   _____
5. Have you ever read an e-book? How does it compare with a traditional book?
   _____
6. What do you read online? _____

LESSON 4

Extra reading comprehension

19 Read the article *Comics: Trash or Treasure?* on page 46 in the Student's Book again. Then answer the questions.

1. What are three reasons people have criticized comics as reading material for young people?
   _____
2. What are three advantages educators see in reading comics?
   _____
3. How have comics been used as a way to communicate social and political information?
   _____
4. How are publishers using comics in Japan?
   _____
5. Where can you buy comics in Japan?
   _____
6. *Spider-Man* is one of the world's most popular comics. How do you know?
   _____

Read the article. Check true or false. Correct the false statements.

Letters to the Editor

Stop Book Banning Now!

From Alicia Vohn, age 16

You might think that book banning is a thing of the past. However, it is certainly not the case. If you are looking for a copy of *Ordinary People* or *The Catcher in the Rye* in my school library, don't bother. Those books have been removed from the shelves. In fact, according to the American Library Association (ALA), since 1990, over 10,000 books have been banned from schools and public libraries around the country. Many types of books: classics, fiction, non-fiction, award-winning books, and even children's picture books have been objected to by angry parents or banned completely, by either removing them from the schools or preventing their purchase.

Why do books get banned?

The reason people give for removing books from school bookshelves is to protect people, especially children and young adults like me, from content that might be dangerous. Most banned books contain violent, religious, sexual, political, or racial content or contain offensive language. Some people think that banning such books will discourage children and young adults from developing bad attitudes, speech, and behavior. But, personally, I don't think young people find words or details in books that they have not yet seen or heard in real life!

Who bans a book?

A "challenge" is a formal written complaint requesting that a book be removed from a curriculum or a library. A book can be challenged by any person or group of people who think its content is inappropriate. Once that happens, a group of experts reviews the book to see if it might be harmful to young people. If they decide that it is, the book is removed. However, schools can ban books without such a review. They just choose not to buy the books at all!

Book banning is wrong and should stop! It's wrong to limit young people's access to books. Book banning limits our freedom to make choices! It stops us from examining different ideas and beliefs and learning to form our own opinions. Schools should teach us to be tolerant of others' ideas and respect our differences. How can tolerance be taught in a classroom that bans books with "unacceptable" ideas?

INFORMATION SOURCE: www.ALA.org

According to the article, . . .	true	false
1. over 10,000 books have been banned in 1990.	☐	☐
2. if a book is banned, it is not allowed in a school or library.	☐	☐
3. people object to some books because their content might be harmful to young people.	☐	☐
4. young people learn offensive language only from books.	☐	☐
5. anyone can challenge a book.	☐	☐
6. the American Library Association reviews challenges against books.	☐	☐
7. a school must wait for the experts' review before it bans a book.	☐	☐
8. a school can ban a book by not buying it.	☐	☐
9. young people should be free to choose what books they can or can't read.	☐	☐
10. banning inappropriate books will teach children tolerance and respect.	☐	☐

21 Read about two books that have been banned from some schools and libraries. Check <u>agree</u> if you agree with the ban and <u>disagree</u> if you don't agree with the ban. Then explain your opinion.

1. *Scary Stories to Tell in the Dark* by Alvin Schwartz is a collection of short stories for children ages nine through twelve. The stories are filled with horror and scary images that are meant to make the reader jump with fear. The collection includes traditional horror tales, contemporary folklore, and scary stories with surprise endings. Beautifully illustrated with Stephen Gammell's spine-chilling pictures, this series is often considered a page-turner that you won't be able to put down. But this series has been listed as one of the most challenged. Many people don't approve of its violence, and parents worry that the stories and frightening illustrations will terrify their children and cause nightmares.

   agree ☐   disagree ☐

   _____
   _____

2. *Bridge to Terabithia* by Katherine Paterson is a story of two fifth-graders, a boy named Jess and a girl named Leslie. Jess is shy, and he often gets angry or sad. Leslie is a talented and outgoing girl who makes friends easily. Once they become friends, the two are inseparable. Jess shows Leslie his love of art, and Leslie shares with Jess her love of fantasy stories. They create an imaginary kingdom, called Terabithia, in the woods where they spend every day after school. Terabithia is filled with imaginary creatures, and while there, Jess and Leslie pretend to fight fears they face in real life. Although many critics consider this book one of the best novels for young readers, it has often been banned because of the disrespect the children show to adults, their impolite behavior, some offensive language, the confusion of combining fantasy with reality, and the death of a child.

   agree ☐   disagree ☐

   _____
   _____

GRAMMAR BOOSTER

A Complete the sentences in your <u>own</u> way. Use clauses with *that*.

1. It's nice *that your children play well together*_____.
2. Many children are afraid _____.
3. Some people are worried _____.
4. Most people agree _____.
5. Until recently, I had never noticed _____.
6. We were surprised _____.
7. I'm disappointed _____.

B Read each sentence with an embedded question. Circle the letter of the underlined word, phrase, or punctuation that contains an error. Each sentence contains only one error.

1. Do you <u>know</u> who <u>she is</u> <u>.</u>
       a.   b.   Ⓒ

2. Could <u>you tell me</u> when <u>does</u> the bus <u>arrives</u>?
         a.   b.   c.

3. I can't decide <u>whether</u> I should <u>go</u> to the movies or stay home <u>?</u>
                  a.   b.   c.

4. <u>Does</u> anyone <u>know</u> who <u>is the author</u>?
      a.   b.   c.

5. Can you remember <u>do</u> <u>they sell</u> newspapers at that store <u>?</u>
                     a.   b.   c.

C. Check the correct sentence in each pair and correct the error(s) in the incorrect sentence.

1. ☐ Let's ask how much ~~does~~ it cost^s?
   ☑ She asked how much it costs.
2. ☐ We're wondering if the baby is a boy or a girl.
   ☐ We're wondering whether is it going to rain.
3. ☐ Can you tell me what is the time?
   ☐ Could you explain what the problem is?
4. ☐ I'm not sure when did they arrive.
   ☐ I want to know when their plane left.
5. ☐ Can you tell me the book is a page-turner?
   ☐ Can you tell me if the book is based on a true story?

D. Rewrite the sentences. Use an infinitive.

1. I don't know what I can do for you.
   I don't know what to do for you.
2. She can't decide what she should have for dinner.
   _____
3. They're not sure whether they should stay or leave.
   _____
4. I wonder when I could call her.
   _____
5. Let me know if I should invite Janet.
   _____
6. Mark can't decide where he should buy a new car.
   _____

E. Use the prompts in parentheses to write sentences with noun clauses.

1. (I completed my article in one day.) _That I completed my article in one day_ is amazing.
2. Let's ask _____ (How much does it cost?)
3. (What did she write in her book?) _____ shocked many people.
4. (This book is a page-turner.) _____ doesn't surprise me.
5. I don't know _____ (Should I read a thriller or a romance novel?)
6. (How did this book become a best-seller?) _____ is a pretty interesting story.
7. Do you know _____ (Who wrote _My Sister's Keeper_?)

WRITING BOOSTER

A Read each sentence. Check true or false.

	true	false
1. A summary of a long reading provides a lot of details about the topic.	☐	☐
2. When you write a good summary, focus on the main ideas.	☐	☐
3. The main ideas of a reading do not give enough information to tell the story.	☐	☐
4. For a short reading, step number one of writing a summary is to identify the details.	☐	☐
5. You should use your own words in the summary.	☐	☐
6. It helps to answer basic information questions about the reading before writing the summary.	☐	☐

B Read the article and answer the questions.

In her 70s, Anna Mary Robertson Moses enjoyed sewing. But as she grew older, it became painful for her. So at age 75, Anna began to paint instead. Many of her early paintings were given as gifts to family members and friends. She also tried to sell a few of her paintings to make a little money. She charged $2 for a small painting and $3 for a larger one.

In 1938, an art collector saw her paintings and bought them all. He was so impressed that he convinced an art dealer to show her paintings in his gallery in New York City. This made many art collectors and museums all over the world interested in her work. She became one of the best-known American artists in the world, with art shows in America, Europe, and Japan.

She became known as "Grandma Moses" and continued to paint until she died at the age of 101. In 26 years she produced over 3,600 paintings. Her paintings show scenes from daily life in rural upstate New York, where she lived most of her life. Some of her paintings were used on Hallmark greeting cards and on U.S. postage stamps. In 2006, a 1943 Grandma Moses painting sold for $1.2 million.

Joy Ride by Grandma Moses

1. What is the article about?

2. When did Grandma Moses begin painting?

3. How did she become a famous painter?

4. What did she paint?

5. How many paintings did she create?

C On a separate sheet of paper, write a summary of the article. Use your answers to the questions in Exercise B.

Reading for Pleasure

UNIT 5 Natural Disasters

Preview

1 Look at the news source. Then check true, false, or no information.

Different cultures around the world have tried to explain what causes earthquakes. Here is one ancient legend from India:

- The earth is held up by four elephants that stand on a turtle's back. The turtle stands on top of a snake. When any of these animals move, the earth moves and shakes.

Source: www.fema.com

	true	false	no information
1. The news source for this information is the Internet.	☐	☐	☐
2. The tsunami caused the earthquake.	☐	☐	☐
3. Three countries were affected by this disaster.	☐	☐	☐
4. This is the worst tsunami ever.	☐	☐	☐
5. The number of dead or injured is increasing.	☐	☐	☐
6. There was no property damage.	☐	☐	☐

2 Complete the conversation. Use the words from the box.

| blizzard | breaking news | casualties | enormous | property damage |

George: Look at this _____1_____ from the north. There was a major _____2_____ there last night. Almost five feet of snow fell.

Christie: That's an _____3_____ amount of snow. That much snow can be dangerous.

George: There was some _____4_____ because of fallen trees. There were also some accidents because of slippery roads. Luckily, there were no _____5_____, just minor injuries.

122

LESSON 1

3 Look at the illustration. What did each person say? Write sentences in indirect speech. Make changes in pronouns if necessary.

1. Dave said _to buy a fast car_.
2. Michael said _____.
3. Julie told him _____.
4. Scott said _____.
5. Lisa said _____.
6. Justin told him _____.
7. Tim told him _____.

4 Rewrite each statement in indirect speech. Make changes in pronouns if necessary.

1. My mom told me, "Heather, go help your cousins."
   My mom told me to go help my cousins.

2. Tina said, "Don't make a mess in the kitchen!"
   _____

3. Sarah told Katie, "Eat all your vegetables."
   _____

4. Rebecca said, "Don't touch my stuff!"
   _____

5. Dad told the kids, "Put away your things."
   _____

Natural Disasters 123

5 Look at the pictures. What is each person saying? Write an imperative in the speech bubble. Then rewrite the imperative in indirect speech.

1. She told the cat _____.

2. The dentist told the patient _____.

3. She said _____.

4. Her dad said _____.

6 WHAT ABOUT YOU? Complete each sentence in your <u>own</u> way. Use indirect imperatives.

1. When I was younger, people told me _____.
2. Our teacher often tells us _____.
3. Today someone said _____.

LESSON 2

7 Complete each sentence with the correct word from the box.

| drought | flood | hurricane | landslide | tornado |

1. When there is a _____, a lot of water covers an area where there usually isn't water.
2. A _____ refers to a long time without rain.
3. When there is a _____, a lot of rocks and earth fall down a hill.
4. A _____ is a storm with a lot of wind that moves over water.
5. A _____ is a storm in which the air moves very quickly in a circle.

8 Complete the conversation. Circle the correct word or phrase in each pair.

Jonathan: I just talked to Gary Feldman on the phone.
Barbara: Oh, what did he (1.) tell / **say**?
Jonathan: He (2.) said / **told** me (3.) don't go / **not to go** to work today. He (4.) told / **said** that he (5.) has tried / **had tried** to go, but he (6.) can't / **couldn't**.
Barbara: Why? What happened?
Jonathan: He (7.) **said** / told that the storm (8.) is / **was** really awful. The roads are covered in ice.
Barbara: Really? I listened to the weather report last night, and they (9.) told / **said** it (10.) isn't / **wasn't** going to be too bad.

9 Change each person's words to indirect speech, changing the verb tense in the indirect speech statement. Use the verbs in parentheses. Make changes in pronouns if necessary.

1. Nick to Joshua (said): "There is a flood in the valley."
   Nick said (that) there was a flood in the valley.

2. Brenda to Aaron (told): "Bad weather was coming our way."
   _____

3. Ryan to Debbie (told): "There's a problem with the car."
   _____

4. Valerie to Daniel (said): "They called me late."
   _____

5. Kathy to Colleen (told): "I'm ready to go any time."
   _____

6. Paul to Doug (said): "Everyone got sick."
   _____

10 Change each sentence from indirect speech to direct speech. Make necessary changes to the tense and pronouns.

1. Ms. Jones told us that the storm was going to be strong.
   Ms. Jones: *"The storm is going to be strong."*

2. Alexa said that the blizzard was coming in our direction.
   Alexa: _____

3. Mr. Kirk said that the weather in the islands had been terrible.
   Mr. Kirk: _____

4. The radio announcer said that a flood covered the roads.
   The radio announcer: _____

5. Howard Denton told me that the hurricane had damaged a lot of houses.
   Howard Denton: _____

11 Rewrite each conversation. Use indirect speech to tell what each person said. Use the correct form of say or tell. Change pronouns and verb tenses if necessary.

1. **Linda:** Terri and I are going to the mall later.
   Stacy: I want to go with you!
   Linda told Stacy that she and Terri were going to the mall later.
   Stacy said that she wanted to go with them.

2. **Chris:** I just got back from Machu Picchu in Peru.
   Theresa: Show me the pictures!
   _____
   _____

3. **Little girl:** Tell me the story about the princess.
   Father: You've already heard that story a thousand times!
   _____
   _____

4. **Joey:** I got the fruits and vegetables at a farmer's market.
   Brooke: They're very fresh and delicious.
   _____
   _____

LESSON 3

12 **Extra reading comprehension** Read the article *Earthquakes* on page 56 in the Student's Book again. Check the statements that are true. Correct the false statements.

☐ 1. The most catastrophic earthquake recorded was in Sumatra.
☐ 2. Severe earthquakes cause casualties, damage to property, and serious economic consequences.
☐ 3. The tsunami in 2004 was caused by an earthquake.
☐ 4. Earthquakes with a magnitude of over 6 on the Richter Scale are generally moderate.
☐ 5. Location can determine the severity of an earthquake just as much as magnitude.
☐ 6. Older-style buildings are safer than modern buildings.
☐ 7. Earthquakes that happen when people are outdoors usually have a higher death toll.

13 Rate the following adjectives from 1 to 5, 1 being the worst.

____ severe
____ mild
____ deadly
____ catastrophic
____ moderate

Did you know?

- Four out of five of the world's earthquakes take place along the rim of the Pacific Ocean, a zone called the Pacific Ring of Fire.
- Most earthquakes last a minute or less.
- Each year, there are about a million earthquakes around the world. But only about 100 of these cause serious damage.

SOURCE: www.earthquakefacts.net

14 Read an article about storm chasing. Then check <u>true</u>, <u>false</u>, or <u>no information</u> for each question.

STORM CHASERS

Tornadoes. Hurricanes. Enormous storms. Just reading these words makes people imagine catastrophic events that can cause countless injuries and severe damages. No one looks forward to weather reports or breaking news that announce these natural disasters. No one, except a small group of about 100 people known as "storm chasers."

Who are these people, and what do they do? A storm chaser is a person who tries to get as close to a severe storm as possible. A few storm chasers are scientists who want to learn more about storms and how they develop. They want to be able to learn more so that someday they can better predict when and where storms will occur. With more information, they could help people avoid the catastrophic destruction and high casualties that often happen when huge storms hit. Others are professional photographers, movie makers, or TV reporters. Some are tour guides who take people close to the center of a storm as part of an adventure vacation. Most are just people who are fascinated by nature and chase storms as a hobby.

Storm chasers travel thousands of miles a week in cars loaded with laptops, cameras, videos, emergency supplies, and a lot of scientific equipment. The most famous storm chases occur in the springtime in an area called Tornado Alley. It is in the Great Plains states of the United States—such as Nebraska, Oklahoma, Iowa, and Texas—where severe storms and tornadoes frequently happen.

Storm chasers study weather data and look closely at the sky to guess the timing and location of storms as they form. They hope to be there when a tornado forms and to follow it as it touches ground. If they are lucky, they will catch a tornado at least once in every five to ten trips.

In 1996, the thriller *Twister* introduced storm chasing to moviegoers. Since then, a lot of people have been fascinated by the topic. There have been TV shows, documentaries, and hundreds of books written about this exciting "sport."

But storm chasing is not for everyone. It is a dangerous hobby. Roads are often wet and dangerous to drive; severe floods can wash away cars; hailstorms can cause injuries and damage to cars; and lightning storms can cause casualties. So why do storm chasers do it? They say that it is amazingly fun, exciting, and always enormously beautiful.

SOURCES: www.stormtrack.org/library/faq/index.htm, www.stormchasing.com, and www.skydiary.com/kids/chasing.html

	true	false	no information
1. Storm chasers look for opportunities to study and photograph huge storms.	☐	☐	☐
2. There are a lot of women storm chasers.	☐	☐	☐
3. There are over 1,000 people who are storm chasers.	☐	☐	☐
4. Storm chasers look forward to tornadoes.	☐	☐	☐
5. Storm chasers know exactly when a tornado will hit a town.	☐	☐	☐
6. There are TV shows about storm chasing.	☐	☐	☐
7. *Twister* is the best movie about storm chasing.	☐	☐	☐
8. Storm chasing is easy.	☐	☐	☐

15 Read the article again. Answer the questions.

1. Why do people become storm chasers? _____
2. How do storm chasers predict when a storm will hit? _____
3. What is Tornado Alley? _____
4. When do storms usually occur? _____
5. Why is storm chasing dangerous? _____

16 Look at the picture. Write about the disaster. What do you think happened? Describe what's happening now.

LESSON 4

17 Put a check next to the words that are examples of emergency preparations and supplies.

- ☐ tornado
- ☐ first-aid kit
- ☐ evacuation
- ☐ non-perishable food
- ☐ flood
- ☐ power outage
- ☐ flashlight
- ☐ battery-operated radio
- ☐ shelter
- ☐ bottled water
- ☐ earthquake
- ☐ other: _____

18 Read the statements from an emergency radio broadcast. Write the letter of the word that is described in each sentence. You will not use all of the words.

_h_ 1. "All residents must leave their homes immediately."
___ 2. "The situation is dangerous, and residents must respond immediately."
___ 3. "The city has been without electricity for four hours now."
___ 4. "Beds have been set up at local schools until people can return to their homes."
___ 5. "Buy items that will last a long time, such as canned beans and tuna fish, in case of emergency."
___ 6. "If the lights go out, you'll need a battery-powered source of light."
___ 7. "Prepare a small set of medications and supplies to treat injuries."

a. shelter
b. matches
c. non-perishable food
d. first-aid kit
e. power outage
f. batteries
g. emergency
h. evacuation
i. flashlight
j. bottled water

19 Read the following brochure. Then check the statements that the article recommends.

A Family Emergency Plan

The thing about emergencies and disasters is that there usually isn't a lot of time to prepare for them. An emergency can strike any place at any time. Is your family prepared?

The best way to deal with an emergency is to prepare for it before it happens. You can do this by making a family emergency plan. Here are some tips on how to prepare one:

• Put a list of emergency phone numbers, including the police, fire, and emergency medical departments, near every phone. Review with children how to call these numbers.

• Make an emergency supplies kit. This should include non-perishable food, bottled water, flashlights, matches, batteries, blankets, a battery-operated radio, a first-aid kit, etc.

• Teach responsible family members how and when to shut off water, gas, and electricity sources in the house.

• Learn basic first aid.

• Decide what you will take and where you will go if you have to evacuate.

• Decide what to do if your family is separated. Choose a place to meet in case you can't return to your home. Pick a friend or family member who lives out of the area to stay in contact with.

• Regularly review and practice your plans.

SOURCE: www.newport-news.va.us

☑ Have a plan in case there is an emergency or disaster.
☐ Write down emergency telephone numbers.
☐ Gather together some things you might need in an emergency.
☐ Show young children how to turn on and off the water, gas, and electricity.
☐ Know how to use the items in a first-aid kit.
☐ Decide when to evacuate.
☐ Find a place for everyone in your family to go if you aren't together.
☐ Practice your plans one time.

20 Complete the indirect speech statements with information from the article.

1. The article says _to prepare_ for an emergency before it happens.
2. The article tells people _____ a family emergency plan.
3. The article says _____ with children how to call emergency phone numbers.
4. The article says _____ where you'll go if you have to evacuate.
5. The article tells you _____ a place to meet if you can't go home.

21 WHAT ABOUT YOU? Are you prepared for an emergency? Which of the following supplies do you have in your home?

☐ bottled water   ☐ non-perishable food   ☐ battery-operated radio
☐ candles   ☐ matches   ☐ other: _____
☐ flashlights   ☐ first-aid kit   ☐ other: _____
☐ extra batteries ☐ fire extinguisher

GRAMMAR BOOSTER

A Read each sentence. If the punctuation is correct, write C. If the punctuation is incorrect, write I and correct the punctuation.

1. Mom said, "D̶on't go in the water." _I_
2. The child said please read me a story. ___
3. I said not to touch anything. ___
4. We told the dog to stay. ___
5. The travel guide tells visitors try to take a tour of the island. ___
6. The woman told her son don't play with your food. ___

B Change each statement from indirect speech to direct speech. Use correct punctuation.

1. The teacher told us to have a good weekend.
   The teacher told us _____
2. Tammy told her assistant to put the mail on the desk.
   Tammy told her assistant _____
3. The waiter said to try the salmon.
   The waiter said _____
4. The actor said not to believe everything on television.
   The actor said _____
5. Mom said not to come home too late.
   Mom said _____

C. Write each direct speech statement in indirect speech. Change the tense only if necessary.

1. Mom just told me, "I need to get some emergency supplies before the storm."
   _____

2. Sarah said, "We bought a new car last year."
   _____

3. Our teacher told us yesterday, "Water boils at 100 degrees Celsius."
   _____

4. His doctor told him, "You need to exercise more."
   _____

5. Last month my parents told me, "We're going to Peru in December."
   _____

D. Look at the pictures. Complete the speech bubbles. Then complete each sentence in indirect speech. Change the verb in indirect speech only if necessary.

1.

    Speech bubble: "I have a terrible headache."

    Jodi just said _that she has a terrible headache_.

2.

    Speech bubble: "You _____."

    Yesterday, the doctor said _____.

3.

    Speech bubble: "He _____."

    Kimmy told her mother _____.

4. Speech bubble: "We _____."

    The coach said _____.

Natural Disasters   131

WRITING BOOSTER

A Read the paragraph below. Add words and expressions to show the order of importance of the details in the paragraph.

It is very important to know what to do in the case of a fire. Fires can be deadly, so knowing what to do in a fire can save your life. _____1._____, look around and locate the nearest escape route, usually the nearest door. _____2._____, if the door is closed, check it for heat before you open it. If the door is hot, do not open it. Escape through a window instead. If the door is not hot, open it slowly to check whether smoke or fire will block your way out. _____3._____, close the door behind you when you leave that room. This can help prevent the fire from spreading to other places and rooms. _____4._____, drop down and crawl towards the exit. It is important not to run or walk as smoke and heat rise. _____5._____, once outside, call the emergency number to alert firefighters to the fire. Sit down and try to stay calm until the firefighters arrive. Never go back into the house.

SOURCES: www.fema.gov, kidshealth.org

B Read the statements about what to do in an earthquake. Organize the statements in order of importance.

____ Check for injuries and damage. See if you can find your way out.

____ Drop to the ground. If you're standing up, you could fall and hurt yourself.

____ Look for a table or another piece of furniture and take cover. This will help protect you from breaking glass or things that fall. Do not move from that place until the shaking stops.

____ When the shaking stops, move slowly away from where you are. Be careful not to trip over fallen objects.

SOURCE: www.fema.gov

C Use the statements in Exercise B to write a short paragraph about what to do in an earthquake. Use words and expression of importance. Begin with a topic sentence. Add more information if necessary.

_____
_____
_____
_____
_____
_____
_____
_____
_____